THE BANTAM
ILLUSTRATED GUIDE TO
EARLY AMERICAN
FURNITURE

THE
BANTAM
ILLUSTRATED
GUIDE TO

EARLY AMERICAN
FURNITURE

MARSHALL B. DAVIDSON

THE BANTAM ILLUSTRATED GUIDE TO
EARLY AMERICAN FURNITURE
A Bantam Book / April 1980

Cover photo by J. L. Houser courtesy of
Freelance Photographers Guild.
Spine photo courtesy of Helga Studios.

Book designed by Lurelle Cheverie

ISBN 0-553-01222-3

PRINTED IN THE UNITED STATES OF AMERICA
0 9 8 7 6 5 4 3 2 1

Contents

Preface

The term "early American furniture" cannot be precisely defined, and there is no very good reason why it has to be. It is a relative term whose meaning changes with the passage of time. Each generation looks at the past from a different perspective. Also, this land was settled in stages over the course of several centuries, and historical perspectives change from region to region. The earliest furniture made and used in New England, the Hudson River Valley, and other old sections of the country is represented by those more or less rudimentary forms, in oak and pine, that are associated with the Pilgrims, the Puritans, and their 17th-century contemporaries. In the middle and farther west, the beginnings of local tradition are reflected by the exuberant Victorian styles of the 19th century that were in favor when these areas were first settled. Emigrants to America following the Civil War may have found their introduction to "fashionable" furniture in the products of Grand Rapids, Michigan, where the ingenious use of mechanical methods of manufacture resulted in new and distinctive styles.

In any case, "early" and "antique" have become practically interchangeable words in popular usage. For customs purposes, in 1930 the federal government ruled that only objects at least one hundred years old could be classed as antiques and thus be admitted into the country duty free. For a time thereafter that ruling was widely construed to mean that an antique was something made before 1830. However, in 1966 another tariff act was passed that clarified the issue. According to this subsequent ruling, any object would be admitted free of duty if it had been made one hundred years or more before the date of entry.

This legal interpretation, of course, puts no limits on the traffic in Americana within the United States. Nevertheless, with its sliding measure of what qualifies as antique it pays some heed to the more flexible view that prevails in the nation's marketplaces where old things are daily bought and sold.

This book deals with virtually all the kinds of furniture that were made in America from the earliest colonial days to the turn of the present century. The text and the illustrations provide practical information that will help the reader identify whatever pieces he may find in an antique shop, an auction room, a museum, or among his own possessions. Comparisons that are made among different examples in the same category, from the most elegant to the most commonplace, enable him also to judge the relative quality of such pieces, be they tavern tables, Windsor chairs, or whatnots.

All these varied forms obviously were made to suit the tastes and needs of the period that produced them. However, each generation discovers merit and interest in furnishings that were discarded by earlier generations as no longer fashionable. In addition, antiques may serve our present household requirements as well as they did those of another age. If this were not self-evident, it would be indicated by the fact that so many different types of early furniture are still being reproduced with some fidelity to original models. Some of these reproductions have been such faithful facsimiles that, although not necessarily made with intent to deceive, they have fooled the experts. At the other end of the range are factory-made versions of "period styles," modified to meet the demands of inexpensive mass production. Often enough, a diligent or lucky collector can acquire a genuine antique for less money than he would pay for such remote, department store descendants—or even for a piece of purely modern design. As a single outstanding example, one of the most elegant pieces illustrated in this book (see Fig. 16, Chapter V) was being used to store pears when it was discovered some years ago by a perceptive antiquarian.

With all this in mind, the forms of furniture illustrated and described in this book are arranged in categories more or less according to the functions the pieces may serve: things to sit, rest, and sleep on; things to put other things in; things to write on, eat and serve from; and, always, things to live with because in general they are pleasant and useful reminders of traditional American values. Such categories cannot always be watertight. In the case of some forms we may find valid uses for which they were not originally intended. Within each category the material is arranged roughly chronologically, from early to late, to demonstrate the progression of styles over the centuries.

As explained in the following historical introduction, some types of furniture, such as court and press cupboards, wainscot chairs, so-called highboys and lowboys, had their day of fashion and usefulness and then were discontinued with the changing nature of daily domestic routine. Other types, such as certain kinds of chairs and tables, chests, clocks, mirrors, and the like, continued to be produced in modified versions throughout generations. As just one example, we can trace the evolution of Windsor chairs such as once graced Mount Vernon and Independence Hall through successive variations of the same basic construction to the relatively homely but eminently practical "kitchen," "firehouse," and "captain's" chairs of much later times. To this day these later versions are produced for use in clubs, board rooms, and offices as well as in households and taverns.

I

Historical Introduction

The earliest colonists to settle along the Atlantic seaboard in the 17th century brought precious little household gear with them. In the tiny ships of the time there was no space to spare for bulky objects. Most of the treasured heirlooms that are said to have come over on the *Mayflower* would have had to hang from the yardarms to be accommodated on that epic voyage. Among the most essential items the emigrants could carry in their luggage were tools with which to make such things as they could not take with them, including tools for making more tools. There was urgent need for settlers skilled in the use of those implements—need for "an ingenious Carpenter, a cunning Joyner, a handie Cooper, such a one as can make strong ware for the use of the countrie," as one early prospectus plaintively explained. Such a one was the Pilgrim leader John Alden, best remembered as the unwitting suitor in Longfellow's legendary poem *The Courtship of Miles Standish.* Alden was actually a cooper charged with maintaining the barrels of "Hot waters" and beer that were deemed necessary provisions for the *Mayflower's* long trip across the Atlantic.

Colonists to new lands always try to re-create the world they leave behind them—those aspects of it, at least, that they best remember and most highly value. So it was with the first settlers along the Atlantic seaboard of America in the 17th century. Very soon after the first trials of settlement were overcome, trained craftsmen were providing their fellow colonists with household necessities—with chests, stools, chairs, and tables, among other things, that in character and in quality were as nearly like those they had known in the villages they had come from as their skills and the material at hand would permit. For a time and in some respects the newly settled world was less new than the world that had been left behind. Eager to continue a familiar pattern of living in a strange and often inhospitable land and cut off from immediate and frequent contacts with developments abroad, the earliest American colonists perpetuated forms and customs long after they had been damned as unfashionable across the Atlantic. In Virginia as well as in New England the first arrivals were for the most part people of modest origins, and the furniture that served their needs was modest in pretension, though by no means crude in workmanship. It reflected a way of life deeply rooted in past experience; it represented not so much a style as a tradition that was carried over from the late Middle Ages.

It is safe to assume that only the best and most durable of the pieces that were produced in these times of beginning have survived into our own day, and few if any of the survivals can be dated before 1650. They are usually rudimentary in form and not highly specialized in function. The chest, for example, was one of the most typical of 17th-century forms. In addition to providing storage space at a time when there were no closets, it might have served as a chair or table as well, and since it was portable to a degree, it could also serve as luggage.

Chairs were not so common as they later became, nor so comfortable. The most conspicuous examples that have come down to us, such as the monumental wainscot armchair with its solid wooden back here illustrated (Fig. 1), made no concession to the irregularities and shifting needs of the human body. They did however impose upon the sitter a measure of dignity. As in the Middle Ages, such massive contrivances were generally reserved for persons of importance. At a time when removable boards set on trestles served as tables, he who occupied the principal seat had the distinction that we recall in the phrase "chairman of the board."

"Wainscot" is a word derived from the Dutch *wagonschat,* referring to a fine grade of oak panel that for centuries was floated down the Rhine from Russia and Germany and exported from Holland to England, among other countries. With its own vast timberlands to draw upon, America obviously had no need to import woods of any description—at least not until exotic materials such as mahogany came into favor in the next century.

The great turned chairs of the kinds said to have been used by the Elder William Brewster and John Carver, of Plymouth Plantation, are hardly less stately or more comfortable (see pages 67–69). Massive chairs of generally similar design and construction were produced in most of the earliest colonies along the Atlantic seaboard. Children and others not privileged to occupy such impressive seats had resort to stools or benches, the supporting members of which were often handsomely and boldly turned (Fig. 2).

The most ambitious and highly developed forms of the period were the press and court cupboards, used for storage and for the display of pottery, pewter, and the like. Toward the end of the 17th century, such large and impressive pieces reached a peak of elaboration (Fig. 3), then for a relatively brief time underwent simplification until, outmoded, they virtually disappeared from the American household. Some other forms from the period, such as the slat-back chair, a traditional provincial type, have on the other hand been produced with variations and modifications over

Fig. 2, WA

the years since, and remote but easily recognizable descendants of early models continue to find a place in today's households (see pages 72–75).

To appreciate the place of such furniture in its original setting it must be remembered that the earliest houses built in colonial America had relatively few rooms and that these were small and low ceilinged. The average 17th-century household consisted of nine or ten persons whose domestic life centered in the principal room, known as the "hall," with its ample fireplace—a diminutive

Fig. 3, HFM

reminder of the great halls of medieval and Tudor English manors. This room-of-all-purpose often served as kitchen, dining room, bedroom, and storage place. The resulting clutter of such interiors can hardly be imagined from the tidily arranged examples preserved in most museums and historical restorations. Under the circumstances privacy and any easy conveniences were at best hard to come by.

Whatever the piece, all the furniture forms that have been mentioned were constructed of straight elements joined together at right angles into uncompromisingly rectilinear designs. The woods most commonly used were oak and pine, from trees which grew abundantly in forests that once covered the coastal areas and reached, seemingly forever, into the hinterland. Maple was commonly used for legs and other turned elements; walnut and red cedar for applied decorations and moldings. Legs and stretchers of chairs and tables were fastened together by slipping the tenon, or tongue, of one element into the mortise, or hole, of another and

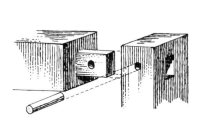

Fig. 4

Fig. 5, OS

by firmly locking the joint with a hardwood pin that was inserted through both (Fig. 4). (In the 17th century such joinery was described as the art "whereby several Pieces of Wood are so fitted . . . they shall seem one entire Piece." It was a construction technique older by far than Christendom.) In cruder versions, chests were simply made of boards or planks held together by wooden pegs or hand-wrought nails. A representative example bears the date 1673, the initials of the owner, and decorative designs of hearts and diamonds (Fig. 5). Throughout the colonial period, it might be added, nails remained relatively scarce and expensive, and played a correspondingly small part in any form of construction. In 1645 the Virginia legislature issued a statute promising the owner who wanted to abandon his house that if he would not burn it down to retrieve the nails, an equivalent number of nails would be provided for his new dwelling. In some early examples of case furniture, the sides of drawers were secured to the front by butting and nailing together the two elements. But

the most common method for years to come was to fasten sides to fronts by dovetailing, that is with interlacing tenons which resemble in shape the tail of a dove (Fig. 6).

Flat surfaces were carved with designs in low relief or adorned with applied turned and split spindles; moldings were simple; but the turnings of chairs and tables, and cupboards were at their best stout and vigorous. Much of this furniture was originally brightly painted with decorative motifs, pitifully little of which can still be found on surviving pieces and is highly prized when it can be, as in the case of a press cupboard, made in New Hampshire about 1700 (Fig. 7). Actually, there has never been a time in American

Fig. 6

Fig. 7, YU

history down to the present day when some forms of furniture have not been painted either with flat color or in decorative patterns. Only occasionally can the makers of such early pieces be identified.

James I reigned in England when Jamestown and Plymouth were founded, and broadly speaking, the designs that have been briefly described are known as Jacobean, after *Jacobus,* the Latin name for James. (For more obvious reasons, furniture of this period is also sometimes called Pilgrim furniture.) They persisted in this country long after that monarch died in 1625, and in the literature of American antiques the term is commonly used to characterize the colonial furniture made throughout most of the rest of the century. Prime examples of these venerable forms rarely appear on the market these days, and when they do they are priced accordingly. Most of those illustrated here have found their way into museums, after some two or three centuries of vicissitudes in private hands. However, long-treasured private collections do come on to the market from time to time and find new individual owners. For the most part these robust forms were made to endure indefinitely, an intention quite contrary to today's emphasis on planned obsolescence. They have suffered from wear and tear over the years—feet and stretchers have been worn thin or altogether away, other details have been broken or lost, the original paint has flaked off or been scoured away or painted over. Careful preservation and restoration has returned many of the finest examples to their pristine state. And here it might be well to point out that a large proportion of the furniture that has survived from earlier centuries, including the finest pieces in museums, has at one point or another been restored to some degree, although this is often apparent only to the most expert eye. "Restoration" and "refinishing" are not necessarily nasty words. It is the degree and sensitiveness of the work that matter most.

For at least half the number of years covered in this book the character of furniture made in America was determined by two major influences. First was the abiding authority of English precedent and fashion; second and equally important was the necessity to adapt such models to conditions of life in the New World. Throughout the colonial period and for some decades afterward, England set the standard in home furnishings—as it did in matters of dress, literature, art, and architecture—that was generally accepted up and down the Atlantic seaboard of America. Even the alien strains that were added to the melting pot from Germany, France, and elsewhere in Europe were affected by the fashions observed in England.

And even as the individual colonies were finally uniting in common cause against the parent government, in some important respects they still had closer ties to the mother country than they had to one another. The tidewater Virginia planters felt more akin to the English country gentlemen than they did to the sharp-dealing merchants from Boston and New York who came to the southern plantations to trade; the cosmopolitan citizen of Charleston, South Carolina, who had studied law at the Inns of Court was in his social outlook at least as close to his London colleagues as he was to graduates of the provincial little college at Princeton, New Jersey. One revealing sidelight on such cultural attachments is that even while George Washington was in the field leading his countrymen in their struggle for political independence, he wrote to the workmen at Mount Vernon instructing them to follow English designs in completing the architectural plans of his mansion on the Potomac River.

However, in spite of a common regard for English precedent, distinctively American strains of design inevitably developed. This resulted from no conscious striving for new manners of expression. It was, rather, a by-product of the conditions of life in the colonial world. One might better say colonial worlds, for from north to south each colony represented a unique situation. Each was born of different circumstances and each was shaped by different historical experiences, often in differing climates. "Fire and Water are not more heterogeneous," observed one European writer, "than the different colonies in North America." The distinctive character of each was marked in its physical appearance, in its social customs, in the nature of its enterprise, and in its separate interpretation of English patterns of living.

Like the seedlings of Old World plants that were also carried overseas by early settlers, before the end of the 17th century imported furniture designs developed fresh variants in their new habitats as a matter of natural course. Village craftsmen working with fading memories of English models served the particular needs of their communities with the skills, materials, and imagination at their disposal and from these ingredients produced local and individual variations of the basic styles of their day. Thus, the carved and painted 17th-century chests made in Ipswich, Massachusetts, differ markedly from those made in the village of Taunton in that same colony, and both types differed from those made at Hadley, Massachusetts, and all in turn from those made in the area about Hartford and in Guilford, Connecticut (see pages 144–47).

A point to be made here is that those local and regional variations in design that were so early apparent continued to characterize American craftsmanship in the changing styles of years to come. For almost two centuries the difficulties of overland travel made waterways the main arteries of communication. Along with freight and news, fashions and styles followed the navigable waters up and down rivers and about bays, creating pockets of local style in the process. Furniture made up and down the Connecticut River, for example, took on characteristics different from those identified with the Massachusetts Bay or the Chesapeake Bay areas or with the Hudson River Valley where Dutch traditions persisted, especially in rural districts, long after the British took over the New York colony in 1664. It is a cherished practice among collectors and antiquarians of our own day to detect and catalogue the differences between a chair or a highboy, let us say, made in Boston or thereabouts and comparable forms made in the same general style in New York or Philadelphia, as indicated later in this book.

As transatlantic trade and travel increased during the course of the 17th century, the impact of English fashions on the colonial scene became more immediate and more insistent. Shortly after the middle of the century those fashions underwent remarkable changes. Following the overthrow of Oliver Cromwell's Puritan protectorate in 1660, the Stuart monarchy was restored to the throne in the person of the voluptuary "merry monarch," Charles II, who had spent most of his years of exile in France. He took as his wife Catherine of Braganza who brought with her from her native Portugal not only the richest dowry in Europe but a host of skilled craftsmen. Then, in 1688, the Stuarts were overthrown with the Glorious Revolution and the Dutchman William of

Orange came to the throne (with his English wife, Mary Stuart). Both monarchs brought in their train fresh ideas from the Continent—ideas that undermined England's old insular traditions and introduced new standards of taste and style.

At the time, Portugal and Holland both stood at crossroads of world trade, and the furniture forms and designs produced in those countries amalgamated influences from all parts of the globe. The international origins of the style that came into fashion can be read in the terms applied to the various elements that distinguished it as a new vogue—"Flemish" scrolls, "Spanish" feet, "Dutch" turnings, and other features taken from a variety of continental sources. More exotic borrowings from far beyond Europe came in the form of real or simulated oriental lacquer for the facing of case pieces (called "japanning" as it was practiced in England and America) and East India–style caning to provide resilient seats and backs for chairs and lounging furniture.

These developments were not simply matters of style; they reflected new concepts of living in which comfort, convenience, and efficiency of household arrangements would play a growing role. A novel variety of chairs, tables, and other types of furniture evolved to serve special needs and purposes—upholstered easy chairs, tables for private dining, writing desks and secretaries, and other domestic equipment that had not earlier been considered necessary to a well-ordered home. In effect, these more specialized forms represented a transition to a modern way of living.

By the end of the 17th century those new styles and ways were becoming naturalized in colonial America. About 1700 one visitor from overseas remarked that there was "no Fashion in *London*, but in three or four Months to be seen in *Boston*." He might have said the same of New York, Philadelphia, and the other busy little Atlantic seaports of the New World. Here the period of transition stretched from about 1690 to 1720, what has long since become known among collectors as the William and Mary period in recognition of the earlier English sources of design. (Actually, Mary died in 1694 and William in 1702.) The heavy rectilinear Jacobean forms were being swept out of fashion and supplanted by furniture of lighter construction and more graceful design. Where it was used, carving incorporated curvilinear elements and was at the same time worked in bolder relief and in more delicate patterns than anything attempted in earlier styles. Nothing could more emphatically demonstrate the radical change in fashion than a comparison of a wainscot chair, for example, with a tall-back, caned chair in the new style, possibly made in New York about 1690 (Fig. 8).

Walnut, maple, beech, and similar hard woods replaced oak for fine pieces. Walnut, particularly, could be easily cut and carved and polished to a fine finish; it was also highly durable and relatively light in weight. The roots and burl sections of the walnut tree were cut in thin slices and used as handsomely figured veneers on case furniture, such as the high chests of drawers and dressing tables that were introduced during this period. In the 19th century these two forms, frequently made in pairs, came to be referred to as "highboys" and "lowboys" respectively. The drawers

Fig. 8, MMA

of such pieces were mounted on legs turned in cup-, vase-, or trumpetlike shapes and bound together by curved stretchers.

It was during the William and Mary period that Americans first came to know and appreciate the solid comforts of a wing chair, or easy chair as it was then called (Fig. 9). No more completely easy chair has ever been devised than this construction with its frame padded on four sides and whose "wings" both warded off drafts and provided a restful corner for a nodding head. Its essential design remains unchanged to the present day. Some idea of its early

Fig. 9, NGA

popularity might be judged by the fact that before the end of the 17th century upholstering had become a busy trade in Boston and other progressive colonial communities. Furniture making had become a thriving business in all the colonies.

The introduction of secretary-desks with the unprecedented conveniences of writing surfaces, pigeon holes for filing, and

Fig. 10, MCNY

drawers for storage incorporated in a single form (Fig. 10) was but one further indication of the more ample and more strictly organized life that was developing in the colonies.

Some of the skilled artisans produced chairs, tables, and other forms that were it not for the use of native woods would be indistinguishable from English imports. However, the extravagantly fashioned furniture that set the style in courtly and aristocratic circles overseas obviously had no place in American life. For instance, such a piece as the oriental lacquer cabinet set in an intricately carved and gilded frame fashioned in 17th-century England (Fig. 11), so characteristic of the exuberance of design during the Restoration, would have been unthinkable in America at the time. In a society where everyone worked, where throughout the colonial period there was no idle class, rich or otherwise, there was no time to waste and little incentive to squander it on the extreme virtuosity that was required to produce the great masterpieces of European furniture. Compared to the examples designed for Hampton Court Palace and the stately English houses, the most elaborate and most meticulously fashioned colonial pieces were relatively simple and modest versions of current styles.

However, in this relative simplicity there was no loss of beauty or usefulness. As the distinguished French visitor to this country Alexis de Tocqueville wrote of the American people, "They will habitually prefer the useful to the beautiful"; but he added, they would also require "that the useful should be beautiful." Long before the word "functional" was coined it could aptly have been applied to typical early American furniture. Tocqueville also remarked on the necessary versatility of American craftsmen who, in a land where manpower was in short supply in the face of the enormous resources that awaited exploitation, had too many different jobs to tackle to specialize intensively in any one of them. Some of the finest early chair- and cabinetmakers also turned their hands to making bread boards, coffins, chicken coops, and similar mundane things for their best customers and their neighbors.

Although Tocqueville's remarks were made in the 1830s his point could be illustrated by examples of American furniture made in the William and Mary style a century and a half earlier. One of the most popular and attractive forms made in New England

Fig. 11, V&A

during that period was the butterfly table, so named because of the wing shape of the brackets that support the folding leaves of the table top. Here is a distinctively American simplification of the stylish gate-leg table of the time. With its raked legs and shapely wings it combines grace and serviceability in an original fashion (Fig. 12). A similar development in vernacular styles appears in American-made versions of the William and Mary chair. From the first introduction of this form into the colonies local and regional variations developed, simplified in design and the more practical for that reason. In some cases, split spindles, or banisters, for the backs and rush for the seats replaced the more costly imported cane. Carving was reduced to a minimum. The last and most enduring of these provincial variations, a far-off descendant of the William and Mary line, came with what was known as the Boston chair (Fig. 13). Commonly made of maple, painted black or red, often upholstered in leather and with curved backs, Boston chairs were both sturdy and comfortable and remained deservedly popular not only in New England but in other colonies as well until the Revolutionary era.

Long before that, a new and radically different style had come into favor, first in England and then by adoption in America. With the death of the Dutch-born William in 1702, the Stuarts returned to the throne in the person of Anne, daughter of the late, unlamented James II. During her reign the alien strains that had been brought into English furniture design so freely in the preceding generation or two were thoroughly naturalized into what has

Fig. 12, BMFA

become known as the Queen Anne style. Every trace of 17th-century stiffness disappeared into a flow of gentle curves. The baroque turnings and complex carvings that characterized the William and Mary style at its height gave way to relatively plain functional elements accented by restrained, judiciously placed ornament. All those earlier borrowed and exotic features were domesticated in a classic harmony of form and function. "In short," wrote Lord Shaftsbury in 1712, commenting on this new concept of design, "we are to carry this remembrance still along with us, that the fewer the objects are besides those which are absolutely necessary in a piece, the easier it is for the eyes by one simple act, and in one view to comprehend the sum or whole."

The single most conspicuous element of furniture construction in this style was the cabriole leg, a form of support originally derived from the profile of an animal's hind leg—a form used in

Fig. 13, WA

Fig. 14

ancient Egypt more than five thousand years ago (Fig. 14). (The term cabriole comes from the Italian *capriola,* a goat's leap.) No other form expressed the spirit of the new style more succinctly and persuasively than the typical chairs of the period, which were designed in a continuous pattern of curved components. Cabriole legs supported horseshoe-shaped seats which gave rise to backs with solid splats modeled to accommodate the curved contour of the human spine and framed by rounded stiles and undulating crests, as clearly seen in an English example (Fig. 15).

As it was interpreted in America, the Queen Anne style remained the dominant vogue from about 1720 (some years after the queen's death) until beyond the middle of the century. In many ways it was the most satisfactory expression colonial craftsmanship ever achieved in furniture design. Forms of every type, characteristically made of solid walnut, took on a simple grace and performed their functions so adequately that we can still live happily with them either in the original or in the copies and approximations that continue to be made. During these middle decades of the 18th century, a growing variety of dressing tables, card tables, tea tables, and other special conveniences catered to changing customs and amenities, and testified to the increasing affluence of the colonists.

In one way or another these "improvements" are related to changing features of domestic architecture. Sometimes, indeed, as in the case of such built-in features as cupboards, architecture and furniture were inseparable. Houses were in general larger than those of earlier generations, and the multiplication of rooms led to increased specialization in household arrangements. Instead of the all-purpose accommodations of the previous century, now there were separate rooms for cooking, dining, entertaining, sleeping, and so forth. From about 1720 until the Revolution, ceilings—in finer homes, at least—were between ten and thirteen feet in the clear (in the 17th century they had often been less than six feet from floor to exposed overhead beams); and with this development tall chests, clocks, and other case pieces could be made larger and topped with bonnets or pediments that repeated the characteristic curve of the period. Looking glasses were also made larger and, with better glass, more revealing. Four-poster beds, not common earlier, rose to new heights as they became more customary equipment.

As in earlier and later years, separate regions of the country produced separate variants of the prevailing fashion, with noticeable differences in their proportions, the nature of their ornament, or some other characteristic of design or construction. Also, as in the case of other styles both earlier and later, the Queen Anne style was quickly translated into vernacular types constructed of local woods, like cherry or maple, that were often of highly individual charm and that continued to be produced in villages far from more sophisticated urban centers long after those centers had turned their attention to newer fashions (Fig. 16).

From about the middle of the 18th century until after the Revolutionary War two major factors influenced the development of furniture styles in the colonies. First was the introduction of mahogany as the primary wood used in the production of the finest pieces; second was the publication in England of a variety of pattern books addressed specifically to the furniture maker and with the working properties of mahogany clearly in mind.

By the second quarter of the century mahogany was widely available in the colonies. The wood, imported from various sources in the Caribbean world, was worm-resistant, almost as strong as metal, and it could be carved in almost any conceivable pattern. It came in a range of attractive colors and the great width of boards that could be obtained made it ideal for table tops and the doors of secretaries and similar case pieces. The various En-

Fig. 16, HFM

glish manuals were imported into America almost as soon as they were published and widely used here.

The Chippendale style is the term commonly used to describe the design of furniture that evolved from the conjunction of these two factors. This is entirely due to the fame acquired over the years by *The Gentleman and Cabinet-Maker's Director,* a manual first issued in London by Thomas Chippendale in 1754. Styles of any kind are rarely created overnight or by a single person. Many of the designs and motifs had originated in England before Chippendale was heard from. However, his was the first of the pattern books devoted entirely to furniture and ornament and fully illustrated. The *Director* went through two subsequent editions. For decades it provided a stimulus to craftsmanship not only in England and her colonies but in other countries as well.

However loosely the phrase may be used, the "Chippendale style" marked a gradual translation into English terms of the earlier French rococo style. ("Rococo" is derived from *rocaille,* a word that refers to the rock and shell forms so popular in French design during the reign of Louis XV.) The resulting effect was one of endlessly curving patterns and asymmetrical ornament incorporating natural and organic forms (Fig. 17). Often a simple engraving in the *Director* would illustrate a chair, for example,

Fig. 17

with different patterns for the arms or legs on either side to suggest how variously separate elements might be used in one or another combination. Some of Chippendale's suggested designs were extravagant to the point of impracticality, a point he himself conceded. Other of his intricate patterns that called for expert craftsmanship were faithfully reproduced in America. As the colonies prospered, more and more highly qualified European artisans were attracted to the New World to practice their crafts there. At times colonial examples are all but indistinguishable from English models. As but one of numerous examples, because it was so elaborately and expertly fashioned, the easy chair illustrated in Fig. 18 was for years considered to be the work of a superior English craftsman. It is now widely believed to be from the shop of Benjamin Randolph of Philadelphia, friend of Washington and Jefferson.

Fig. 18, PMA

For the most part, however, the colonial furniture makers rarely copied any single design from the imported pattern books. More typically, by selectively rearranging separate elements and adding independent contributions of their own, they created unusual native and regional styles. One of innumerable instances that might be cited is illustrated by an engraved design by one of Chippendale's English contemporaries, Robert Manwaring (Fig. 19), and a mahogany chair made in Massachusetts about 1770 (Fig. 20). Here the colonial artisan borrowed almost literally from Manwaring for the chair back, subtly altering its proportions, but substituted graceful cabriole legs with ball-and-claw feet, so popular in America, for the straight, square section legs shown in the Englishman's pattern.

It was in fact during this period that the most distinctive and elegant colonial furniture was produced. The most conspicuous examples are the highboys, especially as this form was developed

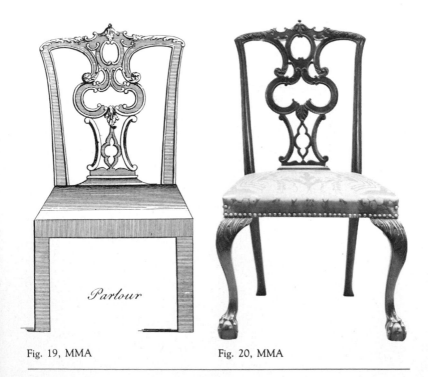

Fig. 19, MMA   Fig. 20, MMA

in Philadelphia, then the leading colonial city (Fig. 21). "After all," wrote Nathaniel Hawthorne more than a century ago, "the moderns have invented nothing better in chamber furniture than those chests which stand on four slender legs, and send an absolute tower of mahogany to the ceiling, the whole terminating in a fantastically carved ornament." Except for decorative details, these ornate pieces with their handsomely carved pediments and elaborate carvings bore no relation to the designs illustrated by Chippendale. Long outmoded in England, the form was here carried to its extreme development. The cabriole leg with claw-and-ball foot so characteristic of these pieces and a hallmark of colonial furniture in the Chippendale style (Fig. 22) is virtually ignored in the *Director*.

Fig. 21, PMA

Fig. 22

Thus, also, the block-front, shell-carved furniture developed in Rhode Island at this time (Fig. 23) seems to owe little or nothing to any of the published design books. Even such details as the finials of highboys and secretaries were of distinctly local design (Fig. 24). How this very sophisticated and unusual style originated and came to such a state of perfection in and about Newport remains something of a mystery. It might be recalled in passing, however, that just before the Revolution, Newport's foreign trade was greater than New York's and that the thriving little city was a cosmopolitan community that supported more than fifty cabinet-makers and woodcarvers, including the Townsend and Goddard families, an extraordinary Quaker dynasty of gifted cabinetmakers allied by marriage and apprenticeship, who are closely associated

Fig. 23, BMFA

Fig. 24

with the development of the Newport "school" of furniture making.

If these examples of the finest colonial furniture spoke with a purely native idiom, so did a long line of derivative forms, notably chairs, which continued to be made of native woods in simplified versions, in naive but often engaging regional, country variations of the high styles of earlier years until well after the Revolution, as will be shown in detail later in this book.

One of the most successful departures from English prototypes, with little relation to Chippendale's designs, came with the development of the Windsor chair (Fig. 25) and related furniture forms. No other furniture form made in America during the course of the 18th century won such wide and enduring popularity. It was a favorite of rich and poor alike; it was used in private chambers and in public places, in state houses and in taverns, in all the colonies. George Washington used Windsors on the porch of Mount Vernon, Benjamin Franklin had them in his Philadelphia home, Thomas Jefferson ordered four dozen for Monticello, and apparently the members of the Continental Congress sat in Windsor chairs as they deliberated the cause of American independence. Quantities of Windsor chairs were shipped to various parts of the world. In a single year just before the end of the 18th century four thousand Windsors were shipped to the French West Indies, five hundred fifty-three to the Dutch West Indies, one hundred fifty-four to the Danish West Indies, and twenty-four to Africa. There was ample reason for such popularity. They were graceful, light, durable, comfortable, and inexpensive. (Washington paid $1.78 per chair for those he ordered.)

Chairs known as Windsors were produced in sizable quantities in 17th-century England. The first American versions were probably made around 1725 in Philadelphia. Regional variants were soon made in other colonies. In their style they all departed markedly from English examples which often borrowed such features as back splats and cabriole legs from the more formal Georgian styles and generally lacked the light grace of American models (Fig. 26). In America the Windsor was an unmistakably native style that bore no relation to the other, more formal styles of the period. In the course of time, variations on the Windsor theme were all but endless—stools, cradles, settees, desk chairs,

Fig. 25, HFdP

Fig. 26

and other forms of the same basic construction, as will be shown later in detail.

Two other "unstylish"—styles that owe little or nothing to the advancing fashions of the day—categories of furniture were introduced into America in the 1700s and continued to be produced here well into the next century: the Pennsylvania German and the Shaker. Each was highly distinctive; the contrast between the two was remarkable. Like the Puritans before them, the Germans from the Rhine Valley and the Palatinate who settled in Pennsylvania in response to William Penn's offer of refuge from persecution in their homeland, came here to preserve and enhance a cherished

Fig. 27, HFM

way of life. What they fashioned in the New World, they made and decorated in the memory of what had served them well at home. These were inevitably modified by American experience and by the proximity of a predominantly Anglo-American culture, but the Pennsylvania Germans clung tenaciously to their basic Old World inheritance—and in some areas still do. They were a conservative and deeply religious folk representing a wide variety of pietistic sects—Mennonites, Amish, Dunkards, Schwenkfelders, among others. The painted designs they applied to dower chests (Fig. 27), boxes, cupboards, and other forms had their origins in folklore and mythology; traditional and often

symbolic motifs that reach back to a distant past. Others reveal a constant awareness of the flowers, the birds, and the beasts which were so intimately part of daily life in field and garden. Unicorns and peacocks, pomegranates and tulips mingle with stars, crosses, and other geometric patterns. The tulip had remained a special favorite, ever since the plant had been introduced into Europe from Turkey in the mid-16th century. The bulbs of these exotic imports commanded huge prices, leading to feverish speculation in which large fortunes were made and lost. Whether the Germans who painted the flowers on their furniture knew that it was an old Persian symbol of love or whether they thought of it as a variation of the holy lily or, grouped in threes, as a representation of the Holy Trinity can only be conjectured.

Fig. 28, PMA

To this robust and colorful kind of furniture, that made by the Shakers stands in the sharpest contrast. Here every semblance of ornament and unnecessary detail was eliminated in favor of purely functional designs, as shown in the chair illustrated (Fig. 28). The Shaker movement began in 18th-century England and was brought to America shortly before the Revolution by "Mother" Ann Lee, a slum-born, illiterate millworker and an inspired spirit, and a small group of faithful followers. Everything produced by the Shakers was a direct expression of the frugal, industrious, celibate communal societies they formed in America. "Whatever is fashioned," one Shaker precept enjoined, "[let] it be plain and simple, . . . unembellished by any superfluities, which add nothing to its goodness or durability." The Shaker societies were at their height between 1790 and about the time of the Civil War, and during those scores of years, while popular fashions were changing radically, frequently, and at times extravagantly, Shaker furniture steadfastly maintained its essential character of functional simplicity carried out with flawless, unhurried workmanship.

During the years that America was preoccupied with the question of its independence, a radical change in furniture design was taking place in the British Isles. The spell of the rococo, the exuberant curvilinear patterns so commonly associated with Chippendale's name, was broken. A new vogue was created, one that found its inspiration in the measured symmetry and delicate grace of models from classical antiquity, such as were depicted in the wall paintings that came to light with the excavations of ancient Pompeii and Herculaneum that were begun in the 1730s and 1740s, and as these were evocatively interpreted in the published designs of the brothers Adam, Robert and James, and other European taste makers of the period. Chippendale worked as a craftsman for the Adams, while the fashions associated with his own name became "wholly antiquated and laid aside." For a half-century to come such classical influences remained dominant forces in furniture design throughout the Western world.

America had to wait until it settled its quarrel with Great Britain before feeling the impact of the new styles. However, with the peace and a resumption of trade with England, that impact was immediate. As in the case of earlier modes, it was through the published manuals intended to guide craftsmen that the neoclassic fashion gained a broad popularity in this country. The most influential of these books were George Hepplewhite's *The Cabinet-Maker and Upholsterer's Guide,* first published posthumously in 1788 and issued in two subsequent editions, and Thomas Sheraton's *The Cabinet-Maker and Upholsterer's Drawing Book,* which appeared in four parts between 1791 and 1794. Interestingly, neither of these men was known as an eminent craftsman in his own day and no single piece of furniture has ever been attributed to either of them. Nevertheless, their names are linked for all time with the forms and motifs recorded in the several editions of their books.

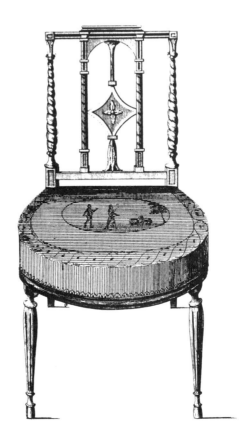

Fig. 29

In the designs of both men, forms became lighter, outlines more severe than had been true of the preceding styles. Carving was subdued in favor of inlay and veneer. Very loosely speaking, furniture with straight, tapering legs square in section, with serpentine lines and with flaring bracket feet (on case pieces) is referred to as being in the Hepplewhite style, as are chairs with shield- or heart-shaped or oval backs and spade feet. Sheraton's influence is acknowledged in square-back seating furniture, tapering, reeded legs, and projecting elements (Fig. 29).

In the finer pieces made during the Federal period (about 1790 to about 1820, when the Hepplewhite and Sheraton styles flourished in this country) delicate inlays and broad facings of exotic woods and painted decoration were marks of elegance. Quite understandably, one of the most popular motifs used for inlays, as well as for other decoration, was a depiction of the American eagle derived from the Great Seal of the United States (Fig. 30). (The later, very popular Hitchcock chairs are "country" types descended from such "fancy" furniture.) Sideboards for dining rooms became fashionable, as did massive breakfront bookcases for other living rooms. One of the most graceful, and most distinctively American chairs ever made was developed during this period, the so-called Martha Washington chair (Fig. 31). Just how it acquired this name no one knows; it was often called a "lolling" chair in its time.

Fig. 30

In the new nation, as earlier in the colonies, American craftsmen occasionally copied imported designs as faithfully as possible, as in the case of a shield-back chair made about 1795 in Salem, Massachusetts (Fig. 32), after a design illustrated by Hepplewhite in one of his plates some years earlier (Fig. 33). Customarily, however, New World artisans chose what elements they would from the imported pattern books, adapting their designs to local and regional preferences and to the artisan's own peculiar skills. Distinctive variations on the prevailing style emerged from each of the more important cities. Such men as Duncan Phyfe in New York, John Seymour in Boston, Samuel McIntyre in Salem, Henry Connelly in Philadelphia, and John

Fig. 31, MMA

Shaw in Annapolis are but a few of the master craftsmen who, each in his way, contributed to the creation of a Federal style in furniture, a diverse American equivalent of Hepplewhite, Sheraton, and their European contemporaries.

In the years following the conclusion of the War of 1812 the neoclassic tradition burgeoned into what was known as the Empire style. Most of the forms in this style are of bolder design, heavier proportions, and stouter construction than the earlier versions of classicism; features that could be seen in the careful renderings of actual examples of ancient furniture shown in the pattern books of Napoleon Bonaparte's French Empire and the roughly parallel versions of the English Regency (as well as in the historical reconstructions of ancient times by such painters as Jacques Louis David). An engraved illustration of an open armchair (*fauteuil*) from the works of the official designers to Napoleon's court suggests the essential nature of this wide-spreading fashion (Fig. 34).

Fig. 32, BMFA   Fig. 33, MMA

Fig. 34, MMA

Development of the style in America was stimulated by the immigration of French craftsmen who came in considerable numbers to such cities as New York, Philadelphia, and New Orleans. In the early years of the 19th century there were more than two dozen French cabinetmakers working in New York City alone. The Scot Duncan Phyfe, who had earlier worked in the Hepplewhite and Sheraton styles, turned to making Empire forms as that style became more fashionable, adding to his considerable fame and his success in business.

Pretentious Empire pieces featured exotic woods and applied gilded metal (ormolu) mounts—features that were quickly reduced at the popular level to painted "graining" and gilding that simulated the more costly materials. This sort of inexpensive but effective "deception" was widely practiced by folk artists throughout the nation for country furniture and architectural decoration. Further simplified by the use of stencils, it was carried over into the ornamentation of mass-produced furniture, such as the popular Hitchcock chairs and Boston rockers.

The classical style lingered longer than any style that was to follow. As late as 1862 at least one English furniture book was still featuring classical designs exclusively. However, by the 1830s and 1840s it was on the wane in America. In the last phase of the revival, the heavy carving, gilded metal mounts, and their simulated equivalents gave way to flat-sawn, often veneered surfaces of almost geometric simplicity. The ubiquitous symbol of this new fashion, which was widely advertised (Figs. 35, 36) and remained in vogue for several decades, was the bold scroll support made in square section and used in various combinations on sofas, tables, chairs, and case pieces. The introduction of steam-driven bandsaws, which could cut out scrolls and other contoured elements from wood of any thickness, brought prices down to a popular level, and the style captured a large market. By this time the classical ancestry of such furniture was all but lost in the simplification of forms that were contrived in the interest of utmost practicality. By this time also, new styles of nonclassical inspiration were competing for public favor.

The progressive democratization of life in America as the 19th century advanced, so colorfully demonstrated in the presidency of Andrew Jackson, and the increasing prosperity of the nation raised confident hopes throughout the land that the material conditions of life would steadily improve for all the people. To meet such expectations for a swelling population, short cuts in production were urgently demanded. Any device that would save time and cut costs, that would increase the workman's daily output, was welcomed and promptly put into service. As a consequence a whole new system of labor-saving machines was developed for sawing, planing, boring, mortising, tenoning, and other operations useful in the manufacture of furniture. Before the middle of the century the Cincinnati Chamber of Commerce was boasting that "every description of furniture, almost from the

Fig. 35, MMA

common bedstead to the most costly articles," was being produced by the factories with steam-powered equipment that were operating in that city. As production soared and prices were reduced Americans at large found it possible to acquire more and more different kinds of furniture than they had ever before thought of owning. Chairs, for instance, which, as earlier explained, in the first years of colonial settlement had been important and prized possessions, were now turned out in prodigious numbers. Wandering Yankee peddlers could offer painted chairs at $1.50 apiece. Americans were not the only customers for such bargains. In 1827 a single day's sailings from Baltimore freighted twelve thousand

Fig. 36, NM

American chairs of all descriptions to points beyond the Horn, where presumably they undersold the local products in distant places. Granted the durability and practicality of such furniture, there must remain at least a scattering of American antiques to be found wherever American ships made their calls about the globe.

Nowhere was the impact of new mechanical methods of production more dramatically illustrated than in the clocks manufactured in the United States during the first half of the 19th century. Considered as furniture, the casings of clocks in general reflected the stylistic trends of successive periods, but these had to be accommodated to the mechanical parts they housed. In no other area of household furbishings is the native American contribution so original, so practical, and so pleasing as in the design and function of clocks. For those with modest purses the price of a case for a tall clock was prohibitive. Early in the 19th century small wall and shelf clocks were being produced in an attempt to provide a modestly priced timepiece; clocks whose designs departed sharply from English models. As an outstanding example, Simon Willard's eight-day banjo clock, his "Improved Patent Timepiece" as he called it, was an immediate success and, despite his patent (granted in 1802), was widely copied (Fig. 37).

No clock could be really inexpensive so long as the brass mechanism had to be laboriously cast, hammered, and finished by hand. When early in the 1800s Eli Terry first manufactured clocks with machine-made wooden works, then adopted the principle of interchangeable parts, and finally reduced his product to the size of his pillar-and-scroll shelf clock, costs came tumbling down. At the same time power-driven veneer and mortising mills and circular saws brought the cost of making cases far below the former level. When another Connecticut Yankee, Chauncey Jerome, adapted the simplified mechanism to the rolled brass that became commercially available in the 1830s, cheap American clocks won markets around the world. In the face of such competition, the Swiss were concerned that they might lose their international preeminence in this area of commerce.

During the several decades preceding the Civil War labor-saving processes assumed a progressively more important role in the manufacture of furniture. The traditional domain of the hand-craftsman diminished accordingly. Particularly in urban centers,

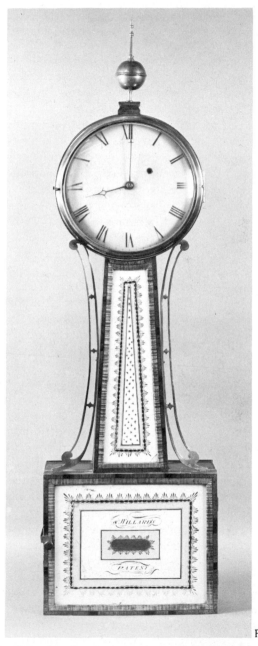

Fig. 37, BMFA

the individual self-employed artisan tended to disappear from the scene. Duncan Phyfe's New York factory, for example, is said to have employed more than a hundred workmen at times of peak production. Under the circumstances, and as communications quickened within the nation, individual, local, and regional variations in style became much less apparent than they earlier had been.

Machine-made furnishings may have lacked the individual refinements of handmade products but they were nonetheless serviceable and, since they were cheaper, they introduced to the average citizen a variety of domestic comforts and conveniences that had previously been restricted to people of more ample means. One consequence of this was the clutter of furbishings we associate with the typical Victorian interior.

The increasing impact of the machine can also be read in the new styles and forms that were developed in the middle years of the century. The relative ease with which wood could be manipulated encouraged manufacturers to produce by mechanical means approximations of what had once required long hours of expert manual labor. As the public at large wearied at last of neoclassical themes, a wide variety of historical styles were revived, or rather were freely adapted in combinations of the forms and ornament of earlier days. It was a romantic age and everything remote in time or place, everything strange or picturesque, everything that pleasantly disturbed the emotions with its mystery, or that excited fantasy, appealed to contemporary taste. The medley of different styles that was introduced paraded under an assortment of names that were often confusing even to those who bestowed them.

The Gothic Revival style, which flourished around the middle of the century, was one of the first to challenge the long-lived authority of neoclassical fashions. For a time, as Gothic cottages sprouted all about the landscape, it seemed that the revival might change the face of America. Generally speaking, the furniture designed for such dwellings bore little relation to any forms known in the Middle Ages. It was a style that by its nature called for inventiveness, especially for dressers, whatnots, bookcases, upholstered furniture and other strictly modern appurtenances that would have bewildered people of the Middle Ages, who were largely unaware of such kinds of convenience, or of any need of them. The anachronisms that were involved in all this imaginative reconstruction were not important. Any picturesque arrangement of pointed arches (Fig. 38), crockets (Fig. 39), cusps (Fig. 40), and quatrefoils (Fig. 41), of towers and turrets and other features associated with Gothic architecture satisfied the current romantic nostalgia for a medieval past that never was. Figure 42 illustrates a chair incorporating a number of these features that was made for Lyndhurst, the large Gothic mansion near Tarrytown, New York, now owned by the National Trust for Historic Preservation. The great advocate of this style was Andrew Jackson Downing, America's leading landscape artist and one of its most discerning critics. He was one of the most influential taste makers of the time and his various books, including those dealing with architectural and furniture design, earned him an international reputation. (In appreciation of his writings, the Queen of Denmark sent him a "magnificent ring.")

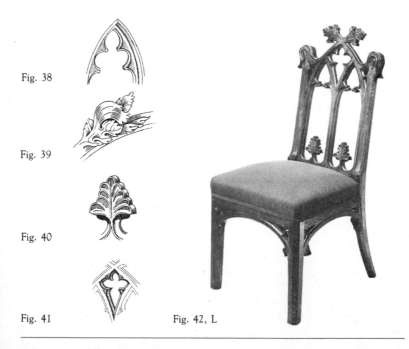

Fig. 38

Fig. 39

Fig. 40

Fig. 41   Fig. 42, L

Fig. 43, HFM

However, Downing himself observed that America at mid-century was in an experimental stage, with a passion for novelty and independence, and that its people seemed determined to "try everything." In 1850, shortly before his tragic and heroic death in a steamboat explosion, Downing observed that the most popular fashion of the moment followed "modern" French designs. He was referring to furniture that was an American adaptation of the French revivals of 18th-century rococo designs—a fashion that was then being "pushed" by such influential publications as *Godey's Magazine and Lady's Book.*

Like the original rococo designs, the style was marked by cabriole legs, sinuously curving contours and waving scrolls. Beyond that, however, the rich, deeply carved detail in the form of clusters of flowers, fruits, and other natural forms in a variety of complicated arrangements was unlike anything known in 18th-century rococo furniture. The application of the new mechanical techniques made relatively light work of such intricately contrived decorative features. Because of its attractive color and figured grain as well as its durable character, rosewood was the wood favored for this style. (It was called rosewood not because of its reddish color but because when freshly sawed it smelled like roses.) French-born émigré furniture makers with names like Seignouret, Roux, Badouine, and others worked in this style in America, although German-born John Henry Belter of New York is the best remembered of the practitioners.

Belter's patented laminating process, in which six or eight thin layers of wood were glued together, counter-grained, and steam-pressed into curved shapes, was a highly successful, substantially effective novelty that was quickly and widely imitated by other manufacturers (Fig. 43). In later years pieces made in this style were commonly characterized as "early Victorian" or, regardless of the maker, as "Belter furniture" (although relatively few surviving examples are known to have been made by him). Inevitably, the high style was quickly modified. The so-called balloon back chair, a simplified derivative of rococo forms, had become a very common type of seating furniture as early as the 1840s, one that remained popular for several decades in a variety of versions (Fig. 44). It is just one more example of how highly sophisticated stylish

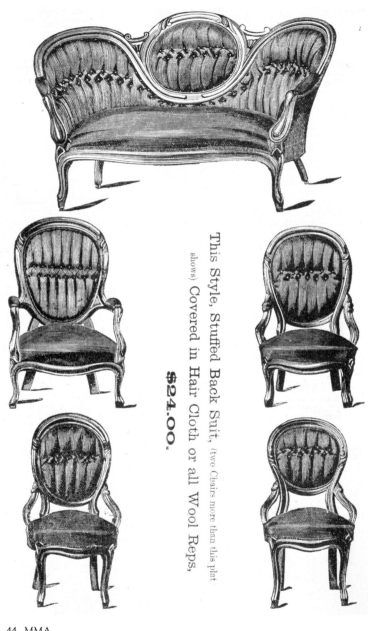

This Style, Stuffed Back Suit, (two Chairs more than this plat shows) Covered in Hair Cloth or all Wool Reps, $24.00.

Fig. 44, MMA

innovations in design of almost every period have been translated into a workaday American idiom.

In passing, to illustrate further Downing's observation that Americans at mid-century were in a mood to try everything, it was during these years that furnishings in cast iron first won public attention. Iron could be cast in virtually any conceivable design and the molds could be used almost endlessly. The supply of iron was abundant; by the 1850s the iron industry in the United States was second in production only to that of England. For the rest of the century a multitude of cast-iron forms were made for use both inside and outside the house. Some of the earliest examples were in the revived rococo style. Generally speaking, the chairs, settees, and other forms followed the style of parlor furniture of the different periods, usually at some distance.

In spite of the evidence presented by the "period" rooms in our museums, probably very few homes—or individual rooms in those homes, for that matter—were furnished in a single style. The middle decades of the century witnessed not so much a progression of styles as a medley of intermingling styles. Along with the rococo there were fashionable pieces in what was called the "Elizabethan" style, characterized by spiral- or spool-turned legs and stiles more or less directly derived from furniture popular during the reign of Charles II and from contemporary 17th-century Flemish designs, generations after the death of Queen Elizabeth. Sometimes elements from a number of different styles were combined in a single piece. In 1850 the celebrated "Swedish nightingale," Jenny Lind, gave a benefit recital in New York for the Widow and Orphan's Fund of the local fire department. The fire laddies expressed their gratitude by commissioning the Brooklyn cabinetmaker John Brooks to make a bookcase for their benefactress. It is virtually a sampler of mid-19th-century design, combining in one piece Gothic, baroque, rococo, Elizabethan, and Renaissance elements as these have earlier been described (Fig. 45). All in all, the different revivals of past styles, variously interpreted, separately and in combination, produced furniture unlike anything known to history.

In his book *Architecture of Country Houses*, published in New York in 1850, Downing illustrated examples of what was termed "cottage furniture," pieces that he deemed suitable for relatively

Fig. 45, MCNY

modest country houses (Fig. 46). Made of cheap softwood, painted in various colors and decorative patterns, these unpretentious forms were derived more or less remotely from current and earlier styles (Fig. 47). Included in that general category are the "Jenny Lind beds," so called simply because their spool turnings were popular when that well-popularized singer was touring the United States in 1850–52 for the master showman Phineas T. Barnum.

Fig. 46, N-YHS

Fig. 47, SHR

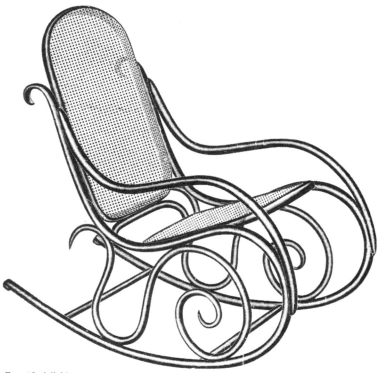

Fig. 48, MMA

One unique type of furniture that owed nothing to traditional styles, the bentwood forms first manufactured by Michael Thonet in Austria about 1840, was introduced into America about the middle of the century and almost immediately duplicated in this country (Figs. 48, 49). It has proved to be one of the most popular and enduring styles in the history of furniture. Exact copies of the early models are still being produced in America as elsewhere.

Another and very different application of the bentwood principle was introduced from the Far East in the form of rattan and wicker furniture, which won wide popularity in the second half of the century and which has also continued in vogue down to our own day (Fig. 50). Such intricately structured pieces had been imported from the Orient from the earliest days of America's

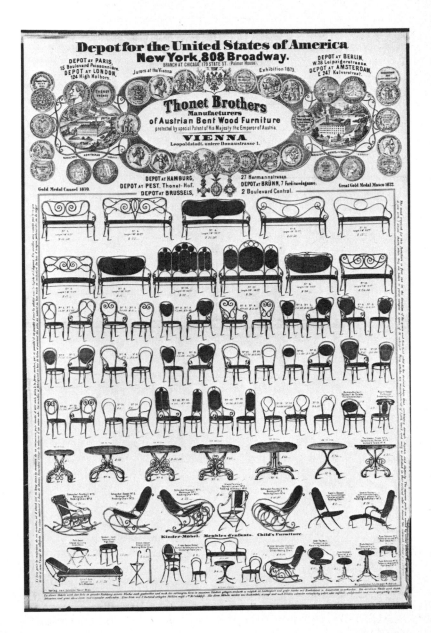

China Trade. Following the Civil War the manufacture of wicker furniture in a wider variety of types was undertaken in earnest in this country. This example dates from 1895. During the postwar decades, bamboo furniture imported from the Far East enjoyed a growing fashion "among people of artistic tastes." Very soon American manufacturers were simulating bamboo with bird's-eye maple. The lathe-turned bamboolike elements were combined in purely Western forms that had little or no relation to the original Oriental designs.

From before 1850 to after 1875, what contemporaries referred to as the Renaissance style maintained a broad popularity. The term covered "almost anything," in the words of one critic of the time. For its purest forms, however, the furniture so called often looked closely to French models of the Second Empire which in turn vaguely recalled the heavier, almost architectural forms of Renaissance Europe. At no time since the Italian and French Renaissance had furniture achieved such massive solidity as it did with this style in the post-Civil War years (Fig. 51).

In spite of widespread factory production craftsmanship of a high order was by no means eliminated. It was in these years that some French furniture firms established branches in the United States, and the most sophisticated work of the émigré artisans vied with the fine products of contemporary Europe. About this time, also, Grand Rapids, Michigan, was recognized as an important furniture-manufacturing center. There and in other cities, west and east, the prevailing styles were interpreted in homely, machine-made versions, as well as in forms in the grand manner. By the 1870s Grand Rapids furniture was finding its way to South America, the Philippines, Hawaii, and Canada, as well as to markets throughout the United States. In their simplified shapes, with almost geometric profiles and relatively flat surfaces, the popular forms thus machine-produced constituted a distinctive style of their own—and were of a quality durable enough to have survived in usable condition until our own day.

Toward the end of the century it was reported that sixty-two furniture manufacturing firms employing nine thousand men were operating in Grand Rapids alone. One of them boasted it could furnish a home for either a mechanic or a millionaire, as occasion required. Although all kinds of wood were used, some of them

Fig. 51, GRPM

imported and expensive, so-called golden oak enjoyed a great vogue; a vogue, it might be added, that is enjoying a flourishing revival in our own time. Among the multitude of forms that were produced, all of them bearing a clear imprint of the machines that spawned them, one of the most typical and memorable was the roll-top desk, without which, it would seem, no office of the 1890s was considered adequately equipped (Fig. 52). In the home the easy chair with an adjustable back that had just been designed by William Morris and his associates in England in the 1860s and that bears his name—the widely appreciated Morris chair (Fig. 53)—enjoyed an enduring popularity.

Fig. 52, HFM

William Morris was one of the English reformers who condemned the machine on principle as a dehumanizing agent and urged a return to the handicrafts. One of the apostles of this new movement in furniture making whose influence was widely felt in this country was Charles Locke Eastlake, another Englishman. His book *Hints on Household Taste* ran through eight American editions from 1872 to 1890. He was not interested in style as such, but rather in what he considered the "honest" and "sincere" constructions of whatever the form, in the spirit of medieval craftsmanship. Thus, he wrote as one of his precepts, "a tenon passing through a mortise-hole and pinned on the other side with a

Fig. 53, V&A

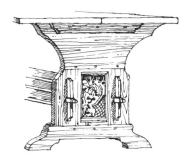

Fig. 54

practicable peg is one of the accepted traits of moral cabinetwork,"
and should be frankly exposed (Fig. 54). True beauty would be
found in the simplicity and usefulness, he maintained.

Such an elementary approach to design made it easy for manufacturers to adopt and adapt his ideas, as they soon did at every
level from the cheapest to the most expensive and meticulously
constructed interpretations. In general, what did in fact become
an Eastlake style was characterized by rectilinear lines, incised
decoration, natural and contrasting wood surfaces, and often a
multitude of turned spindles. It was a stern rebuke to the French
mannerisms that had been flooding the market. To its most ardent
advocates Eastlake's return to original principles amounted almost
to a moral crusade.

The last years of the century saw the emergence of so-called
Mission furniture. Whether the term "Mission" referred to the
primitive furniture turned out by Indian workmen in the Califor-
nia Spanish missions, or whether it implied that the new style had
a mission to perform in radically changing contemporary furniture
design was never clearly defined. In any case, all pretense at
harking back to one or another historical period was renounced.
Mission was hailed as America's first purely native furniture style
(Fig. 55). In the words of Gustav Stickley, who claimed to have
originated it, the new style was based "upon need alone, not the
cultivated taste of the man learned in the great styles of the past,
but the need suggested by the primitive human necessity of the
common folk." Another proponent of the style, who also claimed
to have originated it, was the flamboyant Elbert Hubbard—"Fra

Fig. 55, MMA

Elbertus" as he sometimes called himself, a one-time soap sales-
man and Harvard dropout who, among other miscellaneous activ-
ities, published *The Philistine*, a little magazine which brought him

additional fame by circulating smart sayings and homely apothegms to an enormous audience. His "A Message to Garcia," an inspirational tract published in 1899, attained a total printing of forty million copies.

In their furniture making both men professed a return to hand-craftsmanship founded on elemental structural principles, as the goal of their endeavors. The stark simplicity of the stoutly made, heavy oak forms, fashioned in square-cut patterns and advertised as functional, comfortable, and durable, appealed to the public imagination. Those features also appealed to factories which found them easy to approximate in cheaply contrived and poorly finished reproductions. In one guise or another Mission furniture found a wide market. Examples can still be seen in some of the old libraries and private clubs built and furnished around the turn of the century and, until recently at least, in the benches installed in New York's first subway stations.

II

Chairs—

17th-Century Type

The great boxlike wainscot chairs with solid wooden backs and of uncompromisingly rigid structure were among the earliest types of seating furniture made in colonial America. They were produced in most of the colonies in much the same basic form, with their separate elements joined together by means of mortise and tenon.

These massive chairs suggest baronial dignity but promise little comfort. A cushion on the unyielding wooden seat often provided modest relief for sore-tried buttocks. One of the most elaborate examples has been illustrated in the introduction (see page 3). A more modest version, made in the late 1600s in or near Ipswich, Massachusetts, is nevertheless distinguished by the carved designs of interlacing circles and rosettes of its upper panel and by the carved arcades of its crest rail (Fig. 1). Both pieces have undergone some inevitable restoration over the years, which detracts little if at all from their general appearance or their importance. Another variant of the basic wainscot form, possibly also made in New England, has a back of raised panels and dispenses with carving or a crest rail (Fig. 2). Still another version shows how this essentially medieval form was translated into walnut in Pennsylvania early in the 18th century. The bold turnings of the front stretcher, legs, and arm supports and the crisply shaped crest rail give special distinction to an otherwise plain piece (Fig. 3). In the following years wainscot chairs went completely out of fashion.

Throughout most of the 17th century some large chairs were made with hinged backs that could be lowered onto the arms to serve as table tops. Like the wainscot types, these were typically made of solid oak (and pine), the separate members securely joined together in a stout construction. As in the example here

Fig. 1, BMFA   Fig. 2, YU

illustrated (Fig. 4), such pieces often included a drawer that slid under the seat. Then they served a triple function. These space-saving features were welcome in the small, crowded quarters of the average 17th-century dwelling. (Reduced in bulk such ingenious multipurpose contrivances might indeed serve some of the needs of modern living.)

Fig. 3, MMA

Fig. 4, MMA

The decorative carving that trims the molded stretchers and the pine back, or top (a replacement, but no matter), the shaped arms, and the robust, well-turned legs and arm supports are refinements that make this an outstanding survival. The drawer front of another example with a wide round top and back is incised with overlapping semicircles (Fig. 5). The feet that originally extended below the stretchers have completely worn away, contributing to the squat appearance of the piece. The wear of generations has left a slight hollow in the oaken front stretcher.

Fig. 5, HFM

Great chairs constructed almost entirely of posts and spindles turned on a lathe are among the most venerable relics in early American furniture. The one shown here (Fig. 6), made around the middle of the 17th century of ash and hickory, with tiers of spindles on the back and sides and below the seat, is said to have been owned by Elder William Brewster of Plymouth, who died in 1644. The precious few surviving examples are consequently known as Brewster chairs. A chair apparently owned by John Carver, elected governor of Plymouth under the Mayflower Com-

Fig. 6, MMA   Fig. 7, WA

Fig. 8, CHS

Fig. 9, WA

pact, has spindles only in the back, and similar pieces have been labeled Carver chairs. A very good example in this general category (Fig. 7) displays those pronounced turnings and stout proportions that are considered marks of quality—features that became more attenuated in the course of time until such chairs altogether lost favor with the evolution of quite different patterns of design. A monumental 17th-century chair made of ash and hickory (Fig. 8) represents what is probably the rarest type of early turned chair. The turned spindles of the back relate it to a Carver chair; the two below the seat recall a Brewster. The most unusual feature is the canted back, resting on a turned rail supported by the rear legs.

Throughout much of the 17th century, stools and forms (that is, long benches) served for seating those not privileged to sit in chairs. "Stool" was a general term used to denote a seat for one person; the form obviously could accommodate several sitters at table or in the meeting house. The relative scarcity of such pieces may well indicate the hard use they were put to. In both cases the legs were usually splayed and reinforced by stretchers to insure stability and extra strength. The heavy baluster turnings on the legs of a joint—or "joyned"—stool (Fig. 9) and those of a form (Fig. 10), both dating from the last decades of the century, are characteristic of the best examples that have survived from this early period. The stool particularly, made entirely of maple indi-

Fig. 10, HFdP

cates in its handsomely turned legs how that wood lent itself more easily than oak to such refinements of detail.

In the northern colonies winters were harsher than most of the early settlers had been accustomed to. Settles—that is, benches with tall backs that extended down to the floor, with wings at the sides, and sometimes with hoods—provided protection from chill-

Fig. 11, MMA

ing drafts. One example, probably originating in New England around 1700, is simply made of plain pine boards (Fig. 11); another of slightly later date has a back of fielded panels and shaped side boards (Fig. 12). Such forms were made, with variations, from the 17th through the 19th centuries.

Fig. 12, MMA

Slat-Back Chairs

Whereas the great turned chairs were a vanishing species by the end of the 1600s, slat-back chairs were produced in many parts of the country for centuries to come. The illustrations on these pages barely suggest the endless variations on the basic theme that appeared over the years. An early, massive, and very elaborate example, sometimes called a winged slat-back chair, with its four boldly shaped splats and variously turned and ringed elements, its flat arm rests and rush seat, dates from the last decades of the 17th century (Fig. 13).

A somewhat more typical New England armchair of about the same vintage has only three slats and a less complicated overall construction (Fig. 14), but it is otherwise of kindred spirit—stalwart, enduring evidence of an old traditional design. By the

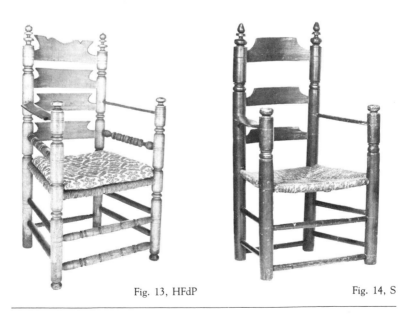

Fig. 13, HFdP   Fig. 14, S

second quarter of the 18th century, chairmakers in the neighborhood of the Delaware River Valley in New Jersey and Pennsylvania were refining that design by increasing the height of such chairs, by lightening their construction, and by arching the slats and arranging them in graduated sizes (Fig. 15). All other things remaining equal, by the standards of today's collectors, the more slats, the more desirable the chair. They were characteristically made of maple and sometimes called "river" or more commonly "ladder-back" chairs. The ringed bulbous front stretcher of the example illustrated is a handsomely turned element that adds further distinction to the design. (Notice that all three examples illustrated have shaped and flattened arm rests.)

As stated above, slat-back chairs were ubiquitous. One country-made version produced in Missouri about 1800, when the population of that section of the country was largely of French descent, speaks with a provincial Gallic accent, noticeable in the lilting curves given to its slats (Fig. 16). Through much of the last century the Shakers turned out slat-backs of spare beauty and, as ever with these religiously dedicated people, of impeccable

Fig. 15, HFM   Fig. 16, MHS

craftsmanship (Fig. 17). The back legs of this chair terminate in rounded buttons neatly fitted into sockets so that the sitter can tilt slightly backward (Fig. 18). The contrast of their light grace with the bulky 17th-century types is just one measure of the wide range of slat-backs that have been produced. During what was termed the Renaissance revival of the 1860s and '70s (see page 54) chairs with slat backs were fashioned in conformity with this very popular and very loosely defined style (Fig. 19).

Fig. 17, PMA   Fig. 18

Late in the 19th century, factories were making great quantities of inexpensive slat-backs as common and useful furniture for kitchens, gardens, and porches. As the new century dawned, Gustav Stickley and his imitators turned out slat-backs of solid oak in the Mission style that was winning favor the country over (Fig. 20).

Fig. 19, HFM   Fig. 20, BM

18th-Century Varieties

A wide variety of chairs made in America between about 1690 and 1730 are commonly said to be in the William and Mary style. This is because their design ultimately derives from the forms that were popular in England during the reign of those monarchs. The armchair made in New York about 1700 (Fig. 21) illustrates some of the basic characteristics of the style: light construction, tall

Fig. 21, HFM

Fig. 22

Fig. 23

back, and intricate carving incorporating C-scrolls (Fig. 22) on crest and stretcher. The arms terminate in ram's-horn hand rests (Fig. 23) above attractively turned uprights. Although cane was often used for the seat and back panels, leather was a durable alternative commonly employed, as here.

In what are called banister-back chairs, split spindles substituted for cane or leather on the back—an agreeable provincial modification of the basic design. The banisters were made by gluing together two pieces of wood, turning them on a lathe, then separating them (Fig. 24), the flat surface facing the sitter's back. Spanish feet are commonly found on chairs (and other forms) of this period (Fig. 25). One very popular version of the style, usually

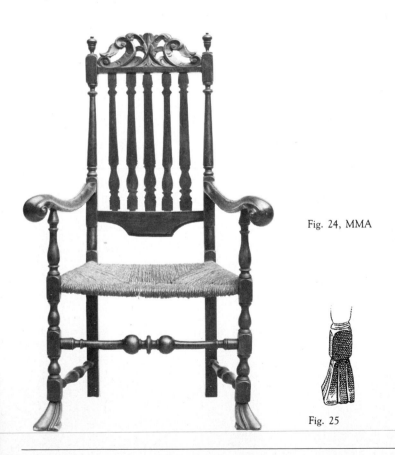

Fig. 24, MMA

Fig. 25

made of maple and painted red or black, has a spoon-shaped back generally covered with leather, as is the seat (Fig. 26). This type of chair was made in or near Boston from the early days of the 18th century and shipped in quantities to other colonies. Known as Boston chairs, they were copied elsewhere, especially in Philadelphia, and remained in vogue well beyond the William and Mary period.

The wing chair, or easy chair, as it was called at the time, was an innovation of the William and Mary period. It was a form that had been introduced to Restoration England from the Continent. Early colonial examples have an arched or shaped crest, horizontally rolled arms, slightly curved wings, and turned stretchers. A

Fig. 26, HFM

typical example (Fig. 27) has rudimentary cabriole front legs terminating in Spanish feet.

Corner chairs, or roundabout chairs, were another development of the William and Mary period. They are sometimes called writing chairs because they were often used at desks. The open front accommodated the voluminous costumes worn by both men and women in the early 1700s. As here illustrated (Fig. 28), early examples of this novel form had no back splats, a comforting feature that was introduced in years shortly to come.

About 1720 chairs in the Queen Anne style began to supersede the earlier designs of the William and Mary period. The new vogue flourished during the second quarter of the century, giving

Fig. 27, NHHS

way after about 1750 only gradually to succeeding fashions. Queen Anne chairs are essentially structural arrangements of curved elements. Stiles of the backs continue in an undulating pattern into the top rail; back splats are typically solid vase shapes, contoured to accommodate the human spine comfortably; seats are often horseshoe-shaped; and front legs are almost exclusively cabriole in design (see pages 19–20), terminating most characteristically in a pad foot. A mingling of the William and Mary and the Queen Anne styles can be seen in a chair probably made in Portsmouth, New Hampshire, by one John Gaines around 1725 (Fig. 29). The back splat takes the vase shape of the Queen Anne manner, but the feet and the turned legs and stretchers retain features of the older styles.

Fig. 28, NHHS

Regional characteristics are often pronounced. A New England maple side chair of about 1730 (Fig. 30) has the spare, slender proportions common to chairs made in that area. The relatively straight stiles of the back and the somewhat narrow splat, the turned stretchers, and the scalloped skirting of the front seat rail are also commonly found on New England chairs. It may be the slenderness of the legs which explains the persistence of stretchers, which were usually dispensed with in more robust types of such chairs.

Philadelphia produced the most elaborate Queen Anne chairs (as well as other furniture forms). An amply proportioned side chair made there about the middle of the century has carved volutes on the back splat and crest rail, shells carved on the knees

Fig. 29, NHHS   Fig. 30, HFM

of the cabriole legs and between the scrolls of the crest rail, front legs ending in trifid feet (Figs. 31, 32), and a nicely curved horseshoe-shaped seat—all characteristic of the finest examples from that city.

An even more elaborate armchair made in that city has a pierced and carved back splat and ball-and-claw feet more typical of the Chippendale styles that were gaining favor in the third quarter of the century (Fig. 33). At the opposite extreme from such sophisticated urban styles, simplified provincial versions of the Queen Anne style have an appeal of their own. Figure 34 represents a type of painted chair that was made in the Hudson River valley at least until the end of the 1700s. The trumpet-

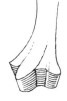

Fig. 31, MMA

Fig. 32

Fig. 33, HMFA

Fig. 34, AIHA

shaped legs, the stiles of the back, and the front stretcher recall the turners' chairs of earlier years; the wide back splat and the pad feet resting on disks are in the Queen Anne style. In another country-made piece, from North Carolina, only the vase-shaped back splat shows the influence of Queen Anne styles (Fig. 35). The piece is a quaint reminder of the way styles of different periods were often ingeniously combined to suit local taste.

Styles in wing chairs underwent only minor changes in the Queen Anne period. The example shown here (Fig. 36), made of walnut and maple about the middle of the century in New En-

Fig. 35, OSR

Fig. 36, MMA

gland, has vertically rolled arms. Turned stretchers are combined with cabriole front legs terminating in pad feet. Corner chairs are now commonly provided with splats and have upholstered seats for the sake of greater comfort; as in the example illustrated (Fig. 37).

Other types of upholstered chairs were contributing to the sitter's ease with the development of the Queen Anne style. The outward flaring arms of one example (Fig. 38), made in New York in the second quarter of the 18th century, were so designed to accommodate the wide skirts worn by ladies at the time. Another type, with a very low seat and known as a lady's chair (Fig. 39), is an early form of what was to develop into the slim-lined, graceful Martha Washington chair of post-Revolutionary days.

Fig. 37, HMFA

Fig. 38, MMA

Fig. 39, HFdP

It should be noted that by this time stools were no longer substitutes for chairs but complements to them. The example illustrated (Fig. 40) has an especially vigorous version of cabriole legs in the Queen Anne style.

Although Queen Anne chairs, both elegant models and rustic versions, were made in colonial America until the last decades of the 18th century, from about 1750 until shortly after the Revolution, designs in the Chippendale style set new standards for the times. In the fully developed style, the curved hoop-back of typical Queen Anne chairs is replaced by relatively straight stiles, often fluted, supporting a yokelike top rail; seats are straight-sided; back splats are commonly pierced and embellished with carving; the knees of cabriole front legs are also often elaborately carved; and the ball-and-claw foot is widely used. All these features are apparent in the mahogany chair shown in Figure 41, made in Philadelphia shortly before the Revolution.

Scores of more or less intricate variations on the prevailing theme were invented in various parts of the country. A side chair made in Massachusetts (Fig. 42) has characteristically lean pro-

Fig. 40, HFdP

Fig. 41, MMA

Fig. 42, HMFA

portions and restrained ornamentation. (Also, it conservatively retains the block-and-spindle stretchers of earlier styles.) One variant type that was made in various colonies has horizontal serpentine slats set between the stiles of the back, usually combined with straight legs of square-section (Fig. 43). They are known as "ribbon-back," "pierced ladder-back," or "pretzel-back" chairs.

Simplified versions of such urban styles were made of native woods all about the countryside of colonial America in the decades on either side of the Revolution. A fair sampling of the

Fig. 43, HFM

different types that were turned out in various sections are shown in the accompanying illustrations. John Townsend, a highly accomplished craftsman of Newport, Rhode Island, at a time when that colony was producing some of the most distinctive American furniture, made the straightforward, well-proportioned sidechair shown in Figure 44. The essential plainness of the piece is relieved by flutings on the front leg and on the "ears" of the top rail. Another side chair, made of maple probably in the post-Revolutionary years (Fig. 45), and painted, is the work of one of the Dunlap family of Chester and Salisbury, New Hampshire. The

Fig. 44, BG   Fig. 45, MMA

design has a personal character not often found in more formal and "correct" examples of the style. In a simpler version, also of maple and from New England, the back splat is solid (Fig. 46). The feet and turnings recall features of much earlier styles. A country-made chair from Connecticut is a forthright version of the elaborately carved ladder-back designs fashioned in urban areas (Fig. 47).

Fig. 46, HFdP

Fig. 47, CHS

Windsors

One witty antiquarian has observed that these light, highly functional forms had "an infinite capacity for taking strains." Although Windsor chairs were made in America several decades earlier, few surviving examples date from before 1760. The term "stick chair," often applied to them, refers to their basic construction, "stick" legs and "stick" spindles driven into a plank seat and held tightly together without nails, screws, or pins. Their components were made of different woods—springy, tough ash or hickory for the slender bows and spindles; hard, close-grained maple for turned legs and stretchers; easily carved pine or whitewood for contoured seats. These elements could be produced in quantity for later assembly, which reduced production costs. Because of this diversity of component woods, both green and seasoned, Windsor furniture was characteristically painted—green, red, black, or whatever. Needless to say, few early examples have survived with the original finish intact. Marks of quality in an older Windsor are a finely contoured saddle-shaped seat (Fig. 48), bold and well-proportioned turnings on arm posts, stretchers (Fig. 49), and legs,

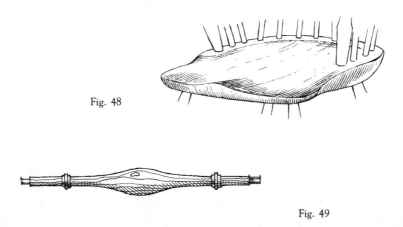

Fig. 48

Fig. 49

Fig. 50

Fig. 51

Fig. 52, PMA

and a marked outward splay of the legs. Generally speaking, the greater the number of back spindles the more highly prized the piece; the chair with nine or, as is found in exceptional cases, eleven spindles is usually a choice specimen. In the case of Windsors with so-called comb-backs, well-carved spiral ears on the cresting rail (Fig. 50) and arms that terminate in knuckle carvings (Fig. 51) are a further distinction.

The chair illustrated (Fig. 52) combines all these features. Other types of Windsors are known by names that are on the whole self-explanatory: bow-back, or loop-back (Fig. 53), low-

Fig. 53, JMML

back (Fig. 54), braced fan-back (Fig. 55). In what is commonly known as the New England armchair the loop back is carried forward and outward in a continuous curve to form the arms (Fig.

Fig. 54, IS

Fig. 55, AIC

56). The most elaborate Windsor form is the comb-back writing arm-chair (Fig. 57). With its broad writing surface and drawer beneath and with an additional drawer under the seat, it is a desk

Fig. 56, BMFA

Fig. 57, NGA

and chair in one. The most modest form is the footstool, often called a "cricket" in the 19th century (Fig. 58). All the examples thus far illustrated date from the second half of the 18th century. The legs of a typical New England Windsor terminate in tapered feet (Fig. 59); Pennsylvania examples often have ball-shaped feet (Fig. 60). In the post-colonial period the legs, stretchers, and spindles were made to simulate bamboo, a practice that continued to satisfy popular taste well into the 19th century. Windsor furniture of various forms, and adaptations of Windsor principles of construction, persisted through much of that century. Low-back armchairs were probably the earliest to be made in this country, and among the latest. Under such various names as "kitchen" (Fig. 61), "fire-house" (Fig. 62), and "captain's" chairs, the later versions were manufactured throughout the nation until our own time.

Fig. 58, HFM

Fig. 59   Fig. 60

Fig. 61, HFM

Fig. 62, HFM

Classical Revivals

Following the conclusion of the Revolutionary War, commerce between England and her former colonies was immediately and actively resumed. Among the items imported by the new republic were the furniture designs made popular principally by the pattern books of George Hepplewhite and Thomas Sheraton. Under this influence chairs became lighter and outlines more severe and symmetrical in the classical manner (see pages 33–37). American craftsmen sometimes duplicated these designs almost literally. A Salem-made chair, probably carved by Samuel McIntyre (Fig.

Fig. 63, HFdP   Fig. 64, HFdP

63), is a faithful but not literal reproduction of a design illustrated by Sheraton. As in the case of earlier styles, innumerable chair patterns were created by varying combinations of motifs, and regional preferences continued in work from different areas. The design of a shield-back chair with a pierced, fan-shaped central splat (Fig. 64) was one favored in New York and in Baltimore. This example is unusual in that it has both inlaid and carved details. The square back of another New York favorite, in the Sheraton style, displays four turned columns forming gothic arches at the top rail (Fig. 65).

What is commonly termed the "Martha Washington" chair, an open-arm chair with an upholstered back and seat, was apparently very popular in the Federal period (Fig. 66). The prototypes of this form are found in earlier French and English examples, but these were outmoded abroad by the time American chairmakers de-

Fig. 65, HFM   Fig. 66, HFdP

veloped modified versions with taller backs and singularly graceful outlines, known at the time as lolling chairs. In this extreme development they constitute a distinctively native style.

During the first few decades of the 19th century chairs in the Hepplewhite and Sheraton style gradually gave way to forms that reflected the influence of English Regency and French Directoire and Empire designs. Illustrations of these were also available in imported pattern books. Essentially these advancing styles were based on a more literal interpretation of ancient classical forms. The back splat of a chair by Duncan Phyfe of New York is carved in the form of a lyre; the front feet are carved paws (Fig. 67). With its saber-shaped legs, curved back rail, and incurved back rest, it recalls the klismos form of ancient Greece, so often seen on vase

Fig. 67, HFdP   Fig. 68, MCNY

paintings of the 5th century B.C. The ultimate model of another chair made by Phyfe about 1810 (Fig. 68), with its "Grecian Cross" legs and brass paw feet, was the folding seat, or curule, used by ancient Roman magistrates.

The heaviness of form and detail that became exaggerated in later phases of the Empire style can be seen in a chair with arms ending in enormous volutes, with four boldly carved and curved paw-footed legs and with gilded details (Fig. 69). From that extreme, in its last phase the classical style was reduced to utter simplicity, as shown in a so-called "gondola" chair (Fig. 70) made in 1837 by Phyfe. Such spare forms were introduced in France during the restoration of the monarchy following the collapse of Napoleon's empire.

Fig. 69, HFdP

Fig. 70, MMA

Fancy Chairs

As earlier noted, there has never been a time in American history when furniture was not painted in one fashion or another. "Fancy" chairs in the Sheraton style—that is, chairs with painted

Fig. 71, PMS

decoration—were advertised in New York in the late 18th century. The back panel of a lightly constructed example made in New England around 1820 displays a freely painted landscape (Fig. 71). Little gilt balls join the bars of the stretchers and the braces of the back. Stencilled designs cover the tops of the dainty flaring legs, which terminate in tiny ball feet. A chair with spirally scrolled armrests, made in New York about the same time, also has stencilled decorations in red and gold together with applied gilded metal ornaments of an Empire design (Fig. 72).

Stencilling was used to simulate such mounts, and also free-hand decoration and carving, on less expensive fancy chairs made during the second quarter of the 19th century. A chair with canted arm posts and a pierced eagle-shaped back splat is both painted and stencilled (Fig. 73). Sturdy, simplified chairs of this general description were mass produced, notably at the Connecticut factory of Lambert Hitchcock, who at one point employed more than

Fig. 73, BG

a hundred workers—including women and children who painted and stencilled—on the assembly line. (Hitchcock's name is popularly given to all chairs of this type.) An example made there between 1825 and 1828 (Fig. 74) carries his mark, "Hitchcock, Alford & Co. Warranted Hitchcocksville, Conn." It has a painted rush seat and was retailed for $1.50.

Fig. 74, HFM

Innovational Chairs

Throughout the 19th century chairs were produced that had little or no reference to prevailing styles, but that were, rather, innovational in their designs. Between 1810 and 1820 Samuel Gragg of Boston produced a kind of chair in which the curved stiles, seat rails, and front legs were steamed into one continuously

Fig. 75, HFdP

curved member (Fig. 75). Examples of these distinctive, graceful forms have brightly painted decoration.

Several decades later, in Austria, Michael Thonet introduced more elaborately curved bentwood chairs that were very quickly copied in America (and have been ever since). A rocking chair made about 1860 (Fig. 76) is an elaborate version of Thonet's original formula. Simpler forms were made in many varieties and used virtually everywhere. Thonet's rockers may have inspired the unknown innovator who, about 1850–60, created a generally comparable version of such delicately balanced forms in iron (Fig. 77). The metal is painted to simulate tortoise shell. This may be a

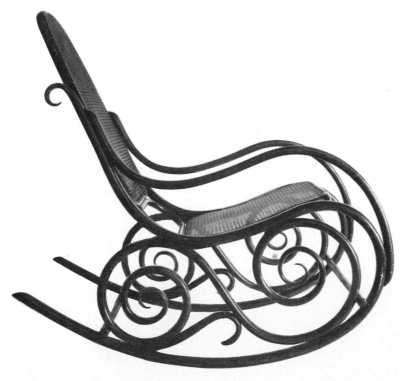

Fig. 76, PC

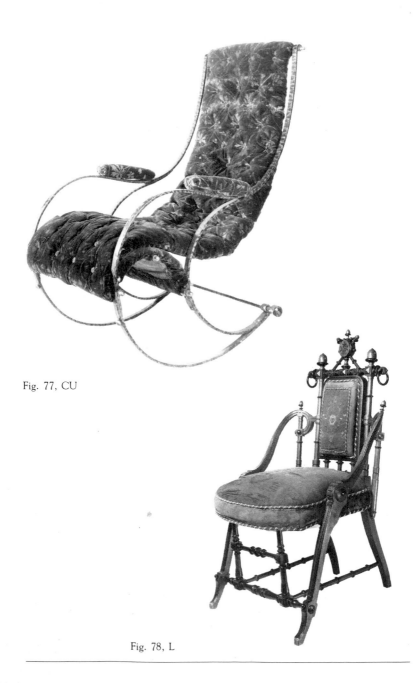

Fig. 77, CU

Fig. 78, L

unique example, but it suggests the growing use of iron in household furnishings of various sorts, as noted elsewhere in these pages. (Roughly similar chairs are being manufactured today for sale in furniture and department stores.) In the 1860s George Huntzinger of New York patented an assortment of chairs of unusual and complicated design, some of which could be folded up and some, like the one here illustrated (Fig. 78), that only appeared to be collapsible. Such novelties were also widely advertised. One book on home furnishing and decoration, published in 1852, pictured a truly collapsible chair that was an obvious forerunner of the type known today as the director's chair (Fig. 79).

The use of metal in the fabrication of chairs led to a number of novel and ingenious designs. In 1849 one Thomas W. Warren patented a reclining armchair that combined cast and sheet iron

Fig. 79, NYPL

Fig. 80, SI

and wood with a spring-based construction (Fig. 80). It was one of many generally similar patented designs, some of which were contrived for use as reclining seats for railroad cars. A garden chair made about twenty years later of painted iron and wire resembles some of the lacy fantasies of Saul Steinberg, translated into a thoroughly functional form (Fig. 81). Although it may well have been made in England, a chair of about 1850 of papier-mâché with

Fig. 81, HFM

ornamental mother-of-pearl encrustations is typical of a fashion that was popular in America at the time (Fig. 82). Papier-mâché is made of paper pulp, mixed with glue or paste, that when wet, can be molded into almost any shape and effectively decorated.

At a far extreme from such elaborate creations, a swivel chair made at one of the Shaker communities exhibits the stark simplic-

Fig. 82, MCNY

ity and rare grace typical of the products of these meticulous sectarian craftsmen (Fig. 83). With its eight curved spindles fitted into a curved rail and a round seat (vaguely reminiscent of a Windsor comb-back chair) rotating on a turned pedestal, and its tapered, cross-arched feet, this type of "turning chair" sold for about two dollars in the 1860s.

Fig. 83, HFdP

In years to come swivel chairs, fitted with casters and adjustable in height, became standard equipment for business and home offices. One example, made of oak and cast iron with a cane seat and back, dates from the 1880s (Fig. 84); turned spindles and incised decorations on the four shaped legs relate it to the more formal domestic furniture of the time. Another example with a shaped seat that recalls those of early Windsor chairs and with square spindles in the back was made about 1900, also of oak and iron (Fig. 85). Both chairs, like many other patented models of the time, could be tilted backward.

Fig. 84, HFM

Fig. 85, HFM

Rocking Chairs

Rocking chairs are typically but not exclusively an American form. There are references to English examples at least as early as the 18th century. Their popularity in this country dates from the early decades of the 19th century. Rockers were of course used much earlier on cradles. (The nurse or servant who cared for an infant was once known as a "rocker.") In the late 18th and early 19th century some old chairs were fitted with rockers. That practice is recalled by a banister-back chair, a reproduction probably made in the 1870s to resemble a colonial piece but designed with rockers such as never would have been originally incorporated in a 17th- or 18th-century chair of this general style (Fig. 86).

Fig. 86, SH

The so-called Boston rocker (Fig. 87), first mass produced in the 1830s in various sections of New England, remained a favorite for years. Made of maple and pine painted black and with stencilled decoration, it was an offshoot of the Windsor chair. The wooden seat curves up at the back, down at the front, and the high back is composed of vertical spindles with a wide, shaped crest rail. What is commonly referred to as a Salem rocker is a slightly smaller version designed, it would seem, for ladies (Fig. 88).

Rockers were made in all styles as the century advanced. The

Fig. 87, HFM

Fig. 88, HFM

Shakers had their own inimitably simple styles. They were probably the first in the country to produce rockers systematically, and they continued to make them through most of the decades of the 19th century both for the use of the Brethren and for sale commercially. A representative example has four back splats, shaped front posts, and neatly grooved runners (Fig. 89). A Victorian lady's rocker, made about 1860–70, is a version of the rococo revival, balloon-back chair of that period (Fig. 90). Abraham Lincoln was sitting in the example shown in Figure 91, a mixture of rococo

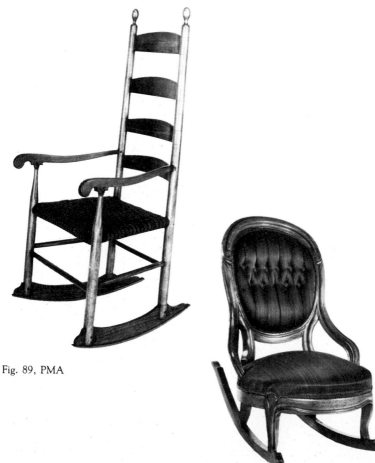

Fig. 89, PMA

Fig. 90, HFM

Fig. 91, HFM

revival and scrolled designs, when he was assassinated. Another contemporary design has a cane seat and back (Fig. 92). The manufacturer claimed it was "inexpensive and sturdy."

A rocker made in Worcester, Massachusetts, in 1876 is typical of a variety of folding chairs that were popular around the time of

Fig. 92, HFM

the centennial celebration (Fig. 93). Countless factories across the land continued to turn out cheap but serviceable rockers of the simplest conceivable design and construction (Fig. 94). Charles Locke Eastlake, dedicated to "sincere" principles of construction, influenced American furniture design, often in ways far from his purpose. A chair that rocked on a platform instead of directly on the floor (known in consequence as a platform rocker) has the

Fig. 93, SI

turned spindles and incised linear decoration associated with his style (Fig. 95). This bulky object was one element in a suite of bedroom furniture, all in the same "homelike style."

What is commonly called wicker furniture became so popular in the decades following the Civil War that in 1886 one reporter described it as "indispensable in modern apartments," as it threatens again to be in our time. (Actually, "wicker" is a catchall

Fig. 94, NGA

term applied to different types of furnishings shaped from fibrous material.) Examples were imported into America from various Far Eastern ports from the earliest days of the China trade. Even earlier, wicker furniture for children was used in 17th-century American homes. According to tradition, a wicker cradle was brought to Plymouth on the *Mayflower*. A platform rocker of painted wicker, made some two and a half centuries later, shows the intricate manner in which this flexible (and all but indestructible) material could be woven about mechanically bent frames (Fig. 96).

Fig. 95, SI

Fig. 96, HFM

Later Historical Revivals

In what has been called the "battle of styles" that raged during the early Victorian period, French influence played a dominant role for several decades. A rosewood chair made in the style associated with John Henry Belter of New York in the mid-19th

Fig. 97, MMA

century epitomizes a vogue that enjoyed wide popularity (Fig. 97). Here a complex abundance of incessantly curving, intricately carved elements revives the spirit of French rococo designs of a century earlier in a freshly synthesized and novel arrangement that constitutes an altogether separate style. Commonly known as Belter chairs, such elaborate forms were made by a number of other craftsmen.

Less exuberant chairs in the rococo style, such as one that is still in the White House and that may have been ordered by Mrs. Lincoln (Fig. 98), more clearly suggest their derivation from earlier French models. The style reached a peak of popularity during the middle decades of the century in the balloon-back side

Fig. 98, WHHS

chair, whose rounded top rail is continuous with incurved uprights, giving the back a roughly balloon-shape outline (Fig. 99).

During those same decades simple, turned chairs classified as what was termed "cottage furniture" provided inexpensive substitutes for the more fashionable forms of the day. The example illustrated (Fig. 100), with painted green and gilt decoration, is

Fig. 99, SHR

Fig. 100, SI

Fig. 101, BM

Fig. 102, BM

from a set of four belonging to a bedroom suite that included beds, bureaus, and other types of related furniture.

As the fashion for furniture in the classical manner waned, new styles gradually emerged, among the earliest of them the Gothic Revival style. Except for suggestive details there is nothing essentially Gothic, or medieval, in any of the chairs made in this style. The graceful side chair shown here (Fig. 101) owes its Gothic "feeling" only to the pointed arches between the balusters and the pierced trefoils of the cresting rail. A dozen chairs of this type were made for the White House in 1846–47 and were later used by Abraham Lincoln in his Cabinet room.

Architects of buildings in the Gothic style often had the furniture for their interiors specially made from their own designs. The elaborate side chair shown in Figure 102, with its pointed arches,

Fig. 103, MCNY

quatrefoil, and crockets, all reminiscent of medieval cathedral architecture, was thus designed about 1840 by Alexander Jackson Davis, a preeminent early American architect, for one of his grandest structures. A simpler version of the style (Fig. 103) was also designed by Davis. A contemporary critic termed these and other pieces designed by Davis "the most correct Gothic furniture . . . executed in this country." Needless to say, the likes of these pieces were never known in the Middle Ages.

Chairs in what contemporaries referred to as the "Renaissance style" were widely popular in the decades just before and after the Civil War. Apparently no one bothered to define the word "Renaissance"; as one critic observed, it "would seem to cover almost

Fig. 104, HFM

Fig. 105, HFM

anything." However, the examples illustrated here (Figs. 104, 105) represent the types that were most commonly given that name. Like the balloon-back chairs, they were manufactured in immense quantities. Legs are characteristically turned and tapered, arms usually flare outward. Walnut was the wood most commonly, but by no means exclusively, used. The pronounced crest on many examples has one or more inset panels of contrasting burl. A typical feature of most chairs in this style is incised linear ornament, sometimes gilded. The chairs were frequently parts of large suites of furniture made for bedrooms, dining rooms, or parlors (Fig. 106).

THIS Solid Walnut Parlor Suit, covered in Haircloth, or any color wool Terry, Seven pieces, $75.

Fig. 106, HW

In the 1870s and '80s bedroom suites were also popularly fashioned of maple turned to simulate bamboo stalks. A chair of that nature, such as the one illustrated (Fig. 107), was advertised for sale in 1876 at a price of $8.67.

In stark contrast to the medley of styles reviving others of the European and ancient past, the 19th century ended with the introduction of Mission furniture. This was a style based uncompromisingly on four-square functional forms made, at the start and

Fig. 107, MMA

at their best, of solid oak (Fig. 20). In the beginning Gustav Stickley, an originator and ardent promoter of such forms, called them collectively craftsman furniture. Here, he believed, was a return to first principles in design and construction. Such a native, fundamental simplicity would, he further believed, very likely never go out of fashion as so many other styles had done over the years past.

Fig. 108, BM

The English reformist designer, William Morris, had earlier called attention to these first principles of honest construction and good taste and with these, and his own physical comfort, in mind had brought about what became known as the Morris chair. A metal rod that could be fitted into any one of a number of notches in the rear supports of an armchair made it possible to raise or lower the hinged back to various levels that promised ease (Fig. 108).

III

Chests & Boxes

The chest is the oldest of known furniture forms. It was an essential item in the earliest colonial households, and its importance is indicated by the elaborate carved and painted designs with which so many surviving examples are ornamented. One such, here illustrated (Fig. 1), belongs to a group

Fig. 1, BMFA

of generally similar chests made in or near Essex County, Massachusetts, in the years around 1675; a number of them are attributed to Thomas Dennis of Ipswich, a craftsman of that town. The panels, stiles, and rails of the front are completely covered with variously colored shallow carvings combining late Tudor and Jacobean motifs.

Fourteen plain panels set within a molded framework appear on all four sides of another oak chest of about the same date (Fig. 2). This unusual arrangement suggests that the piece could have stood free from the wall, to be seen from all sides.

For storage of small objects, boxes were almost as indispensable as chests and often were no less abundantly decorated (Fig. 3). They are commonly referred to as bible boxes, since they no doubt served to house the Scriptures as well as other treasured possessions. Spices were precious commodities frequently stored in small chests under lock and key (Fig. 4). The interior is lined with a series of little drawers, and it rests on bun feet, so characteristic of case pieces of the period. Both the box and small chest shown here

Fig. 2, SI

Fig. 3, BMFA

Fig. 4, HFdP

are associated with Dennis because of the nature of their carved designs. (The spice chest is dated 1679 and bears the initials *TH*, presumably for one Thomas Hart, a village neighbor of Dennis in Ipswich.)

Although chests of framed and paneled construction, the elements joined by tenon, mortise, and dowel pins were customary in the 17th century, simpler chests consisting of six flat boards fastened together by pegs or nails continued to be made into the 18th century. The front plank of a representative sample, inscribed with the date 1702 and the initials of its owner, has molded decorations and gives way to a single drawer at the base, with

Fig. 5, BMFA

knobbed pulls (Fig. 5). It was made in New England of pine, rather than oak, and the end boards were continued down and shaped to serve as feet.

Decoratively painted chests and boxes continued to be fashioned until well into the 19th century in many parts of the country. Examples made by the German pietists who settled in Pennsylvania are well known. A chest made about 1780, probably in Berks County, displays a number of the traditional ornamental motifs favored by these earnest folk; the unicorn (symbol of purity), the dove (symbol of conjugal bliss), the ubiquitous tulip, and so on (Fig. 6).

Fig. 6, MMA

Another chest from the Hudson River Valley, where Germans also settled, with a trestle base and dated 1765, is covered with so-called oyster patterns which at either end surround heart-

Fig. 7, SHR

shaped designs (Fig. 7). A box made earlier in the 18th century, also in colonial New York, is colorfully ornamented with stylized tulips and other floral forms (Fig. 8). What could be imagined as a

Fig. 8, SHR

swirl of "eyes" decorate a blanket chest made in New England probably about 1820–40 (Fig. 9). Some of such pieces were painted by itinerant professionals, others by local amateurs, usually females who had available to them books of art instruction to guide their efforts. A sea chest, probably made in Massachusetts early in the 19th century, is appropriately ornamented with nauti-

Fig. 9, OS

cal motifs (Fig. 10). Like other chests of this sort it is slightly wider at the base to ensure its stability in rough weather, it has a high base molding to keep the bottom clear of a wet floor, and it has rope handles passed through a wooden bracket screwed to the sides of the piece.

Fig. 10, HFM

The early, low chests sometimes doubled for a seat as well as a storage space. The addition of drawers reduced the one function and augmented the other; it also led to a variety of new forms used for stowing away clothes, fabrics, and other materials, as will be seen in the following pages.

A large number of late 17th- and early 18th-century chests with drawers have been traced by characteristic decorations to specific localities or areas in New England. Some details of a multi-drawered carved and painted example with applied, turned and split spindles (Fig. 11) are comparable to those that appear on identified Dennis pieces made in his Ipswich shop. The painted tendrils may have been meant to simulate, or suggest, the elaborate inlays then popular in England. If the piece is the work of one

Fig. 11, HFdP

man, he would have been a turner, a carver, and a painter, as well as a joiner. It is dated 1678, the earliest known dated American chest of drawers.

Several distinctive types of chest were made in separate localities along the Connecticut River valley. Late in the 17th century in the neighborhood of Hartford, chests were made with highly stylized tulips and sunflowers carved on the panels, usually above a pair of drawers, and with applied spindles and bosses stained black to simulate ebony. The one shown in Figure 12 is highly typical of these so-called sunflower chests. (The floral motifs may in fact have been developed from the Tudor rose and the Scotch thistle.)

Fig. 12, BMFA

Farther up the valley, in the vicinity of Hadley, Massachusetts, another special variety of chest with drawers evolved, decorated with all-over flat carvings of vines, leaves, and flowers, characteristically painted red, black, or shades of some other color and outlined by thin incised lines against a matted background. The piece illustrated (Fig. 13) is one of more than a hundred known survivors of these Hadley chests, as they are called. To the south,

Fig. 13, NGA

in and near Guilford, Connecticut, bordering the shores of Long Island Sound, another type developed toward the close of the 17th century. Known as Guilford chests, these display painted rather than carved designs, the motifs drawn from Tudor and Dutch sources (Fig. 14).

In Boston and its environs around the turn of the century panelled chests of drawers were made in two sections, the forerun-

Fig. 14, MMA

ners of the tall chest-on-chest that became popular in the later years of the 18th century. As in the example illustrated (Fig. 15), the front feet are given the shape of flattened balls, or bun feet. Brass pulls in the form of tear drops replace the wooden knobs commonly used on 17th-century furniture. Each successive period was to have its characteristic form of brass hardware. Designs of representative examples from successive periods are illustrated in Figures 16–32.

Fig. 15, BMFA

Furniture Hardware

The designs of drawer pulls and keyhole escutcheons used on early American cabinetwork changed from one period to the next along with the changing styles of the furniture itself. Those examples here illustrated are characteristic of the many varieties that will be found on pieces appearing in this book.

Figs. 16–19   Late 17th–early 18th century

Figs. 20, 21   First half of the 18th century

Fig. 22   About 1720–1780

Figs. 23, 24   About 1765–1810

Figs. 25, 26   Late 18th–early 19th century

Fig. 27   About 1810–1830

Fig. 28   About 1840–1875

Fig. 29   1860–1875

Figs. 30, 31   1870–1880

Fig. 32   1885–1900

To eliminate the inconvenience of bending down to reach into a low chest, the storage compartments were sometimes raised on supporting frames or stands with turned legs. A simple example made in Massachusetts in the last quarter of the 17th century has a shelf nailed to stretchers connecting the legs (Fig. 33). A more

Fig. 33, BMFA

Fig. 34, MMA

elaborate chest-on-frame, painted black, with a hinged top and a drawer (Fig. 34) more clearly represents what is in effect an intermediate step between the low chest and the lofty highboy that became so widely popular as the 18th century advanced. Another example of the same form, probably made in the late 1600s, has spool-turned legs and stretchers and the case, or chest section, is divided into narrow panels divided by cross pieces with applied bosses (Fig. 35). The chest and its underpinnings are a single unit; with time these forms would consist of two separate units.

Fig. 35, AIC

IV

Highboys & Lowboys

By the end of the 17th century the chest-with-drawers on a legged stand had started its evolution into a high chest of drawers, commonly called a tallboy in England and in America later to be known as a highboy. In America the form persisted longer than it did overseas and it was here that it developed characteristics unprecedented in English examples. A dressing table, later termed a lowboy, was at times associated with the highboy as a companion piece, although each was also made separately.

An early example of a colonial highboy, probably made in the Hudson Valley late in the 17th century, combines five spirally turned legs—harking back to European styles of the period of Charles I and Charles II—connected by flat, shaped stretchers common to furniture of the William and Mary period (Fig. 1). A highboy more typical of the developed William and Mary style has six cup-turned legs, these also united by flat, shaped stretchers, terminating in flattened ball feet with deep supporting pads (Fig. 2). In common with much case furniture in this style the flat, front surfaces are faced with decorative veneers and the drawers are edged by rounded moldings. A lowboy, also made in the first decades of the 18th century and in the same general style (Fig. 3), shares features with the lower section of such highboys; the flat

Fig. 1, MMA

Fig. 2, HFM

stretchers (here crisscrossed), the scalloped skirting, and two deep drawers flanking a more shallow central one. Here trumpet-turned legs support the carcass. With minor variations of detail, these cup turnings (Fig. 4) and trumpet turnings (Fig. 5), both obviously so called because of their suggestive shapes, are notably characteristic of such standing pieces of the period.

Separately made highboys and lowboys of the succeeding Queen Anne period shared common characteristics in similar fashion. A lowboy of curly maple, probably made about 1720–1740 in or near the Connecticut Valley, shows lingering traces of earlier styles in its shaped skirt with pendant knobs and in its modified Spanish feet; but the cabriole legs, the carved fan, and the molded edges of the drawers (now arranged in a different formation) are all in the Queen Anne manner (Fig. 6). A Connecticut highboy made of cherry at approximately the same time

Fig. 3, HFM

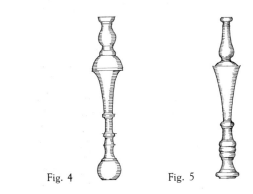

Fig. 4   Fig. 5

Fig. 6, BMFA

has very similar stylistic features (Fig. 7). The detachable arrangement surmounting this piece is stepped to permit the advantageous display of pottery or porcelain, a device that apparently was peculiar to America. Few of such "Steps for China ware," as they were noted in early documents, have survived the years.

Highboys in the more fully developed Queen Anne style took on an almost architectural character, rising to a broken-scroll pediment graced by ornamental carved finials (Fig. 8). An example made in Charlestown, Massachusetts, in 1739 has fluted pilasters flanking the veneer-faced drawers (Fig. 9). Both pedi-

Fig. 7, HFM

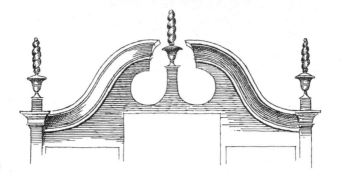

Fig. 8

Fig. 9, BMFA

Fig. 10, MMA

ment and pilasters recall details common to buildings of the time. A matching highboy and lowboy (Figs. 10, 11) are unusual pieces in that they are japanned, that is, painted in a very approximate imitation of oriental lacquer work, with gilded raised figures distributed against a simulated tortoise shell ground. The best japanning was done in Boston, where these pieces were made around the middle of the century. Aside from this exotic decoration, however, this pair represents typical Queen Anne design.

Fig. 11, MMA

Fig. 12, MMA

The basic form of highboys and lowboys changed little in the Chippendale period, but regional variations in design introduced different and distinctive treatment of detail. Philadelphia produced the most elaborate versions in the years surrounding the Revolution. A representative matching mahogany highboy and lowboy (Figs. 12, 13) are enriched with rococo carvings in an abundance not matched in the ornamented examples of other colonies. Ball-and-claw feet are used exclusively. Highboys had been outmoded in England some years before these pieces were made in America, without ever having reached such an extreme development.

Fig. 13, MMA

For some reason very few highboys in the Chippendale style were made in the New York region, and when they were produced the design was remarkably simple compared with Philadelphia models (Fig. 14). Those made in New England were also on the whole relatively restrained in their design. Newport, home of a school of highly skilled cabinetmakers, produced highboys of

Fig. 14, BG

simple and distinctive grace. A closed bonnet-top, bird's-claw front feet (sometimes with undercut talons) combined with pad feet on the back legs, and a handsomely carved shell with its edges contained within an arched reserve are typical features of the fine highboys coming from that very enterprising coastal town (Fig. 15).

Fig. 15, HMFA

In some inland New England villages local craftsmen, using native woods, created highly individual patterns in highboys, as well as in other forms of furniture. In East Windsor, Connecticut, Eliphalet Chapin adapted the ornate Philadelphia style to local taste and his own skill. In a cherry highboy that he probably made, the intricate rococo carvings in the Philadelphia manner have been reduced to a few intertwined tendrils on the top and bottom central drawers and a central "sea horse" cartouche interrupts the plain latticework of the pediment; aside from inset quarter columns the piece is otherwise undecorated, and no less appealing for that (Fig. 16). Another highboy of "tiger stripe" maple made in New Hampshire, probably by a member of the Dunlap family of

Fig. 16, WA

Chester and Salisbury, is both more elaborate and more provincial in its interpretation of the Chippendale style (Fig. 17). The usual pediment has been converted into a fretwork gallery with carved fans, three half-shells surround the double scrolls of the skirt, and the tall two-sectioned case stands on squat cabriole legs with thin ankles. All in all this piece represents one of the most distinctive regional expressions of the Chippendale style in provincial America (Thomas Chippendale would have wondered how his name could ever be associated with such a piece), and one of the last of the highboys to be made here. In the years following the Revolution the popularity of the form waned and it went the way of the great cupboards of earlier days to extinction.

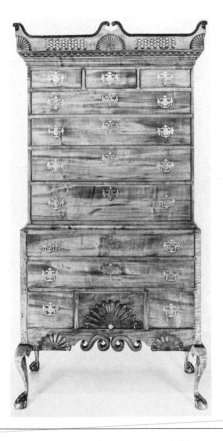

Fig. 17, HFdP

V

Chests of Drawers & Chests-on-Chests

B y the opening years of the 18th century the chest of drawers had become well established as a distinct furniture form, and as the century advanced it was to become a more widely used household convenience than it earlier had been. Later in the century the double chest, or chest on chest, also grew in popularity.

A New England chest in the William and Mary style from the early 1700s has drawers that are veneered with walnut burl and that are edged with double-arched bead moldings (Fig. 1). The turned ball feet resting on deep pads are characteristic of the period (Fig. 2). The piece illustrated in Figure 3 could be classified either as a chest of drawers on a frame or an incipient highboy. In any event, it is a country-made form, probably dating from the second quarter of the 18th century, that ingeniously combines stubby cabriole legs with pad feet in the Queen Anne manner and

Fig. 1, BMFA   Fig. 2

Fig. 3, OS

a deep, shaped skirt reminiscent of William and Mary styles. The bulging rounded molding of the cornice (known as a torus molding) conceals a separate drawer.

With the Chippendale period both the chest of drawers and the chest on chest came into their own. In Rhode Island, superlative craftsmen of the related Townsend and Goddard families created a

Fig. 5   Fig. 6

Fig. 4, BMFA

regional style in these forms, as in other types of furniture, that appears to have had no distinct precedent in European models and can probably be considered a distinctively American innovation (Fig. 4). The salient characteristics of their cabinetwork were the blocked arrangement of the front, the handsomely carved shells on the uppermost drawer (Fig. 5), and the carved whorls that curl onto the curved bracket feet (Fig. 6). A simpler version of block-front design that with minor variations was used in various sections of the country in the production of chests of drawers is often found with a recessed central section—a "kneehole" type, as books on antiques refer to them for obvious reasons. These are sometimes also called dressing or bureau tables, but they remain essentially chests of drawers. The example illustrated (Fig. 7) was

Fig. 7, BMFA

Fig. 8, BMFA

made in New England, near Boston no doubt, in the Revolutionary period.

Where the development of the chest on stand had relieved the householder of bending over to get at the contents of a low chest, the impressive height of the chests-on-chests, as of many highboys, now imposed the difficulty of getting onto a chair or stool to place anything in the upper drawers. With its molded scroll pediment and corkscrew finials, a massive specimen made in Marblehead, Massachusetts, in 1780 (Fig. 8) rises to a height of more than seven feet (and there were taller ones). The drawers of the upper case are flanked by fluted pilasters with bases and capitals in the classical style; the drawers of the lower case gently undulate in an ox-bow shape, scarcely noticeable in the illustration, but adding a subtle grace to the actual piece.

An otherwise plain chest, also from Massachusetts and also made of mahogany, is distinguished by a similar curved front that is accentuated by the corresponding curves of its molded, overhanging top (Fig. 9). In some New England chests of drawers in

Fig. 9, BMFA

the Chippendale style curves entirely take over the carcass, which swells out from top to bottom on both sides and the front in what is called a bombé form (Fig. 10). A Connecticut chest-on-chest made of cherry by one Reuben Beman, Jr., of Kent in the years following the Revolution has a pinwheel carving on its uppermost central drawer—a motif repeated in miniature as terminals for the scroll pediment (Fig. 11). The pediment also features delicately shaped openwork designs and cone-shaped finials. Drawers are arranged in nine tiers of graduated depth. A distinctly different version of the chest-on-chest apparently was favored in the neighboring New York area. Samuel Prince, a Manhattan cabinetmaker, illustrated on his labels an example very similar in style to

Fig. 10, BMFA

Fig. 11, HFdP

Fig. 12, BMFA

the piece here shown (Fig. 12). Instead of the more usual scroll pediment on such pieces, the overhanging cornice in this case is flat and ornamented with dentils, a series of little rectangular blocks, projecting over a band of fretwork. Both the upper and lower cases have inset quarter columns and are separated by a rippled molding.

As ever, in towns and villages at some distance from urban centers chests, like other forms, were made of native woods in provincial versions of the high style of the time. The relatively simple example shown in Figure 13 was undoubtedly made by one of the Dunlaps of New Hampshire. Members of this family also

Fig. 13, YU

Fig. 14, HD

fashioned chests on chests very similar to the highboy illustrated in Chapter IV, Figure 17. Much earlier in the century some unsung country cabinetmakers fashioned an unusual chest on chest with twenty-four drawers in the upper section and three large ones below, all resting on stout bun feet and painted (Fig. 14). It was designed to house the varieties of herbs, simples, and other medicaments of an apothecary. A much smaller and more sophisticated chest also has an abundance of small drawers and compartments to serve a similar purpose (Fig. 15). Made in the south near the turn of the century, it may have been the first aid kit of some rural plantation owner.

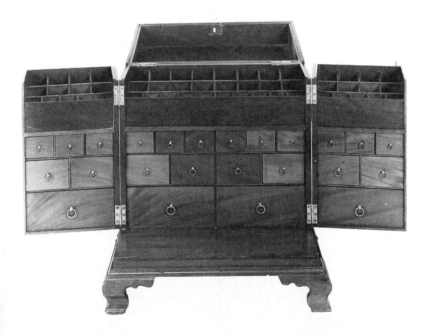

Fig. 15, MESDA

Like the highboy, the chest-on-chest went out with the close of the 18th century. One of the last American examples of this form, and the most opulent, was made in Salem, Massachusetts, in 1796

Fig. 16, BMFA

by William Lemon with carvings by Samuel McIntyre (Fig. 16). (When it was rediscovered a drawer of this piece was being used for ripening pears.) Standing more than seven and a half feet tall to the top of the little carved figure of Nike, Greek goddess of victory, in the broken triangular pediment, this piece mingles classical with Chippendale features. McIntyre's carved ornament, although classical in spirit, is a highly personal statement. It should be recalled that at this time Salem was a prosperous port, celebrated around the world for its maritime ventures. Its merchants were rich and could afford furniture made "in the best manner."

A New England bow front chest of drawers made early in the 19th century has delicate inlaid stringing bordering the top and the base and gracefully flaring bracket feet, often called "French feet" at the time (Fig. 17). Chests of drawers were now becoming

Fig. 17, BMFA

known as bureaus. In this piece the influence of Hepplewhite's designs is clearly apparent. Another chest of drawers, or bureau, also from New England and with a slightly bowed front but standing on turned legs rising to reeded columns fitted into circular projections at the corners of the top, is the Sheraton-style equivalent of the same type of furniture (Fig. 18).

Fig. 18, BMFA

Generally speaking, a piece of furniture can be dated from the latest feature it displays. By that prescription the chest of drawers illustrated in Figure 19, with its delicate inlays and oval brasses, would have been made late in the 18th or early in the 19th century. The slim cabriolelike legs are vestiginal reminders of Queen Anne styles from many years earlier.

Fig. 19, AAAM

VI

Dressers &
Bureaus

O ne of several new forms introduced in the classical revival
period was the dressing chest of drawers with an attached
mirror, a useful kind of bedroom furniture that became
widely popular in the Victorian period. (Free-standing dressing
mirrors that were placed on chests or tables had been used through
much of the 18th century.) The mirror of an early example made
in Boston during the Federal period, about 1810–20, is supported
by a scroll frame (Fig. 1). Two banks of drawers are veneered with
bird's-eye maple. The mahogany legs and corner columns are
round, reeded, and turned in the Sheraton style. Another new
form of the time was the semicircular commode. In the example
shown here, from about 1800 (Fig. 2), the four drawers are flanked
by compartments that swing on brass hinges. It is an altogether
elegant piece, also from Boston, made of various contrasting
woods and with projecting colonettes in the Sheraton manner.

A later example, made in New York about 1830, displays the
heaviness of form and detail characteristic of the full-blown Empire style (Fig. 3). Instead of inlaid designs, the decorations on the
drawers are stencilled in gilt, a time- and cost-saving expedient
that has its own charm. The stout pillars terminating in huge
lion-paw feet with sharply delineated claws (Fig. 4) and the

Fig. 1, BMFA

Fig. 2, BMFA

Fig. 3, MWPI

lyre-shaped mirror supports are highly typical of design in this period.

About the middle of the century, dressing bureaus in the so-called "cottage" style were produced in quantities. An example made in Philadelphia is of native wood gaily painted black and gold with polychrome floral designs (Fig. 5). The piece is, in effect, a Victorian extension of Sheraton "fancy" furniture.

To adapt the form of a dressing bureau to the Gothic revival style required ingenuity and inventiveness, both of which qualities were boldly exercised in the creation of the massive example here illustrated (Fig. 6). The carved cusp and crockets and the pointed arches were details borrowed from the vocabulary of medieval cathedral architecture to create a nostalgic mood in an otherwise thoroughly "modern" piece of furniture. The rococo revival, a style contemporary with, but totally different from the Gothic, had its own version of the dressing bureau. In New Orleans, which had a special appreciation of such French-inspired designs, a master craftsman, probably of French descent, fashioned the example illustrated in Figure 7. The focus of the piece is its oval mirror framed in a succession of alternating curves and both supported and crowned by additional curved elements.

The same general spirit enlivens a tall bureau turned out by a Cincinnati factory about the time of the Civil War (Fig. 8). The elaborate frame of the mirror, which can best be called a superstructure, largely consists of intricately composed, pierced scrolls and is topped by a very substantial cresting. It represents a

Fig. 4

Fig. 5, PMA

Fig. 6, SI

Fig. 7, HCHS

Fig. 8, NM

type of furniture that we can justifiably call Victorian. In another massive bureau fashioned in what was rather vaguely referred to as the Renaissance revival style, the exuberance of the curved elements has been somewhat restrained in favor of a more solid appearance (Fig. 9). It is handsomely made of satinwood and

Fig. 9, TRB

rosewood as part of a bedroom suite and represents what was considered the height of fashion in the 1870s.

A walnut dresser with an adjustable mirror (Fig. 10) demonstrates how the reliance on steam-powered, mechanically operated tools translated the Renaissance style into an inexpensive,

Fig. 10, HFM

mass-produced equivalent of the finest examples. The flat surfaces and simple incised floral ornament are typical of such furniture at this level of production. Most of the later dressers, at any level, were made as elements of a bedroom suite of related pieces. A bureau of imitation bamboo, made of turned maple (Fig. 11), was designed as an element in such a suite, described in the 1880s as "unique and cheerful." A tall chest of drawers in the same general style suggests the close relationship of various elements in such an assemblage (Fig. 12). The dresser illustrated in Figure 13, an example fashioned about 1880 of blond maple, was also designed en suite with other pieces of bedroom furniture. Inset tiles on the little cabinets with their galleries of spindles that flank the bureau's mirror are translations of designs recommended by the English reformer Charles Eastlake. Eastlake also pointed out that the natural grain of wood, without "artificial varnish," as here displayed, was itself an ornamental feature.

Fig. 11, MMA

Fig. 12, MMA

Fig. 13, L

VII

Cupboards, Wardrobes, & Whatnots

T he most ambitious furniture forms produced in colonial America in the 17th century were the massive press and court cupboards, used both for storage and for display of pottery, pewter, and silverware. With its various turned and ebonized applied elements and its carved drawer fronts, the press cupboard illustrated here (Fig. 1) provides a summary statement of the Jacobean style as it was interpreted in New England. The applied ornamental shapes that appear on the doors and panels of this piece, known as strapwork and "jewelwork," had enjoyed popularity in England since the time of Queen Elizabeth I.

Another type of cupboard, somewhat smaller and known as a court cupboard from the French word *court,* meaning short, has an open shelf beneath the enclosed section (Fig. 2). By the end of the 17th century these impressively large forms were becoming an obsolescent fashion to be succeeded by chests of drawers, chests-on-chests, lowboys and highboys, and other more specialized forms. In some country districts, however, reduced and simplified versions continued to be made until well into the next century. An example of painted pine made around 1700 in eastern New

Fig. 1, BMFA

Fig. 2, BMFA

Hampshire (Fig. 3) shows such a provincial press cupboard, a late survivor of a vanishing species of furniture.

The typical large storage piece used by the Dutch who settled along the Hudson River Valley and adjoining areas of the middle colonies was of a totally different kind, modeled on the great, high-standing cupboards of their homeland. The best of these European examples were heavily carved with representations of

Fig. 3, BMFA

fruits and flowers or elaborately inlaid (Fig. 4). In the New World, such opulent ornament was sometimes reduced to painted imitations of figures in relief (Fig. 5). Such decorations may well have been the first still-life paintings done in America. These wardrobes commonly have a heavy, overhanging cornice. The two doors in the front conceal a series of shelves inside. The kas, as such a piece was called (from the Dutch *kast*), was also made,

Fig. 4, MMA

Fig. 5, MMA

unpainted, with paneled doors and stiles (Fig. 6), ornamented with applied, faceted bosses. This one dates from the second half of the 17th century. By the early years of the next century, those relatively elaborate forms of decoration gave way to simpler designs (Fig. 7). The kas, too, was on its way to extinction.

Generally similar forms were made in New Jersey and Pennsylvania throughout the 18th century. A Pennsylvania German example (called a *schrank* there) is dated 1779 and is decorated in

Fig. 6, AIC

wax inlay simulating the inlay of rare woods (Fig. 8). Commodious cupboards made with two sections, either with open shelves (Fig. 9) or shelves behind glazed doors in the upper part for the display of tableware, were also characteristic of the typical Pennsylvania-German household in the latter years of the 18th century and the early years of the 19th. In its fluted corner columns and the dentils of its cornice moldings, the example

Fig. 8, PMA

Fig. 9, HFdP

shown in Figure 10, from about 1750, suggests the influence of the more formal styles of English descent as these were followed by urban craftsmen in the Philadelphia neighborhood. However, the persistence of Pennsylvania-German folk patterns is evident in another, brightly painted cupboard dated 1828 (Fig. 11).

The early French settlers of the Midwest also carried with them the traditions of their homeland. Figure 12 represents a wardrobe or *armoire* in the provincial French style of the 18th century. Made of walnut in St. Louis about 1780, its decoratively carved fleurs de lis, as well as its generally Gallic character, stamp it with a sharp French accent. Another American-made armoire, made about 1820–40 in the area of Louisville, Ohio (like St. Louis, also an early haven for French-born settlers), is made of local poplar wood painted and stained to simulate the graining of more expensive woods (Fig. 13).

Fig. 10, PMA

Fig. 11, NGA

Fig. 12, MHS

Fig. 13, HFM

A mahogany linen press made in New York around the time of the Revolution in a regional version of the Chippendale style is closely related to the secretaries and other cabinet pieces from that area (Fig. 14). The essential difference is, of course, that the

Fig. 14, SHR

interior of the upper section of the press is fitted with shelves and drawers for storage purposes.

The pine cupboard illustrated in Figure 15, made in New England probably just before the middle of the 18th century, with

Fig. 15, HF

Fig. 16, MMA

its fielded panels and the decoratively scrolled framework encasing its shelves, has an almost architectural character. Cupboards actually built into the architectural fabric of a room were in fact becoming an increasingly popular feature of interior design as the 18th century progressed. The free-standing triangular corner cupboard shown in Figure 16, with its fluted pilasters, classical moldings, and panelled doors, undoubtedly bore a close relationship to the woodwork of the room in which it was originally installed.

A mahogany wardrobe made in New York about 1830 has stencilled designs in gilt, roughly approximating the metal ornaments applied to the most elegant examples of furniture in the

Fig. 17, MCNY

Fig. 18, OS

Empire style (Fig. 17). It may well have been one element of a bedroom suite, as were other wardrobes designed in the styles of ensuing periods.

Far removed from such modishness, two early cupboards probably intended for use in a kitchen offer straightforward accommodation for the display and storage of practical household gear. The elongated C-scrolled sides of one made around the beginning of the 18th century (Fig. 18) recall similar outlines of settees of that period. An unusual feature of the other (Fig. 19), made of pine in

Fig. 19, SHR

New York in the second quarter of the century, is the absence of any backing to the shelf area. Shaped sides and feet are the only concessions to style.

Food safes, storage cabinets with decoratively pierced tin doors designed to screen any access of vermin and insects to pies, pastries, and other edibles, were common to 19th-century kitch-

Fig. 20, NGA

ens, particularly in the Midwest. The piercing of the tin, as in the two examples here illustrated (Figs. 20, 21), was often skillfully patterned. Both are apparently of Texas origin.

The whatnot developed to cope with that profusion of gewgaws and knicknacks we associate with a typical Victorian parlor. (Periodicals of the day explained that whatnot was the equivalent

Fig. 21, SAM

of the French *étagère.*) It won popularity in the American home around the middle of the last century, and in their general design such pieces were adaptations of the prevailing styles. The elaborate tracery of one example, designed to fit in a corner, incorpo-

Fig. 22, BM

rates motifs in the Gothic revival fashion—pointed arches, trefoils, and so forth (Fig. 22). The lower section has mirrored doors.

An abundance of sawn scrolls of another whatnot, probably made in the 1860s, recall the enthusiasm of those years for

Fig. 23, PMA

Fig. 24, HFM

rococo-revival designs (Fig. 23). Fret-cutting machinery, recently perfected, encouraged the display of such intricate patterns. Still another example, made about the same time, with mirrored panels and towering to a height of more than seven feet, has the arched cresting associated with what was called the Renaissance-revival style—a term that had very little specific meaning (Fig. 24).

Special racks to hold music sheets and books, known as canterburies, were introduced in England as early as the 1780s. An American canterbury, made in New York about 1823, is a representative example of this form, although it is without the usual partitions that divided the rack into two or more sections as recommended by Sheraton (Fig. 25). Such parlor conveniences remained popular throughout the century, as seen in a late exam-

Fig. 25, HFdP

ple, factory-made of flat-sawn, incised elements very roughly suggesting Renaissance-revival styles (Fig. 26).

In a wicker catalogue of 1895 the four-tiered music stand illustrated in Figure 27 was advertised for sale at $14. Sewing baskets,

Fig. 26, HFM

or seamstresses' work stands comparable to one shown here (Fig. 28) sold for $5 or $6—for slightly more if the piece was shellacked, stained, or enameled.

Fig. 28, BM

VIII

Desks &
Secretaries

Colonial

Until the end of the 17th century colonial writing furniture consisted largely of portable desks, that is, boxes with hinged slanting fronts that could be placed on tables, as had been true throughout the Middle Ages when the form was sometimes known as a scholar's box. The interior space was used for writing materials, books, and related paraphernalia. Figure 1 represents an example from the late 1600s.

Fig. 1, NGA

Fig. 2, WA

Fig. 3, MMA

During the William and Mary period a new form developed in which such a box was set upon legs of its own, that is to say, upon a standing frame made especially to accommodate it. In the two examples of such desks-on-frames here illustrated, the sloping writing surface lifts upward, as in the case of the desk box. One, made of pine and maple, is a relatively rude piece, in spite of its nicely turned legs and the moldings of the rim that secure the box in place (Fig. 2). The other is in every way a superior piece, with elaborate and unusual turnings, a scalloped and ornamented skirt, and more complicated moldings (Fig. 3). It was made of gumwood in New York around the turn of the century, probably by or for someone of Dutch descent, judging from an inscription inside the lid that is illegible but clearly in the Dutch language.

A next step in the evolution of the desk was to marry it to the chest of drawers, so to speak, providing a much more commodious piece of furniture, and to hinge the lid so that it fell forward to rest on sliding supports. A highly characteristic example of this development, made about 1700, is veneered with walnut burl, stands on large ball feet (Fig. 4). It and the following example

Fig. 4, HFM

have teardrop drawer pulls typical of the period. The interior of the writing compartment has ten pigeonholes and five small drawers. A more elaborate type of writing furniture that appeared

Fig. 5, CW

about the same time was the secretary, a much taller piece constructed in two sections whose entire upper front panel, at this early stage in the evolution of the form, dropped outward to provide a writing surface (Fig. 5).

The desk-on-frame never did go entirely out of fashion after it was first created in the 17th century, although it naturally underwent stylistic changes from period to period. Early models in the William and Mary style gave way to forms typical of the Queen Anne period, as neatly expressed in an example made about 1735–50 of walnut, probably in Virginia, with its graceful cabriole legs resting on pad feet, its suavely contoured skirt, and its otherwise very simple outlines (Fig. 6). In a small, country-made version of the same period, the cabriole leg is barely suggested and

Fig. 6, HFdP

Fig. 7, HFdP

Fig. 8, BMFA

the upper section consists of three drawers beneath the writing compartment (Fig. 7).

Essentially the same form was continued in the following, Chippendale, period, differing only in details; often with some carved ornament on the knees of the legs and with characteristic ball-and-claw feet (Fig. 8). Chippendale's designs also illustrated furniture with straight, square-sectioned legs often with a block foot, known as Marlborough legs (Fig. 9), as seen in this example made in Philadelphia shortly before the Revolution (Fig. 10). A

Fig. 9

Fig. 10, HFdP

later, country-made version of the desk-on-frame recalls the earlier examples reduced to the utmost simplicity (Fig. 11).

Slope-front, or slant-top desks with a series of drawers beneath the writing compartment, and secretaries increased in popularity as the 18th century progressed and, like other forms, often displayed regional characteristics. A desk of curly maple made in New Hampshire in the middle years of the century stands on short cabriole legs with pad feet in the Queen Anne manner (Fig. 12). This otherwise plain piece is enlivened by the tiger-stripe pattern of the wood, much prized by collectors. If its surfaces are not

Fig. 11, S

tampered with, maple furniture takes on an attractive and inimitable dark honey color.

The secretary, a form that provided drawer space, a writing compartment, and a storage place for books and documents, assumed new importance in the Queen Anne period, an importance that did not diminish for many years to come. An example made in Newport about 1730–50 has a flat top, arched panel doors typical of the time in pieces of this kind, and plain bracket feet (Fig. 13). The one relief to the general plainness is the blockfront and shell design construction of the interior of the writing section,

Fig. 12, HFM

an early instance of what was to become a celebrated feature of Newport cabinetwork by members of the Townsend and Goddard families, as seen on a chest of drawers, from about 1760, illustrated in Figure 14, and on the superb secretary shown in Figure 23 in the Introduction.

Not all furniture made in Newport in the Chippendale period was so richly developed. A slant-top desk made there about the same time as the secretary just cited is a straightforward example, without embellishment—the basic form of such a desk and nothing more (Fig. 15). In 1769, at Colchester, Connecticut, one Benjamin Burnham (who inscribed within the piece, "sarvfed his time in Felledlfey") made a cherrywood desk with leaf-carved cabriole legs, a block front, and an unusual three-tiered bank of interior drawers of robustly curved design (Fig. 16). An itinerant, like other colonial craftsmen, Burnham combined several different regional features in this one piece. In its pierced lattice pediment and inset, stop-fluted quarter columns, a Connecticut-made secretary, also of cherry—a wood favored in that colony—again shows the influence of Philadelphia workmanship (Fig. 17). As a touch of elegance the capitals, bases, and stop-flutings are of brass, as befitted a piece made for a colonial governor, as this one was, probably by Eliphalet Chapin of East Windsor.

Fig. 14, BMFA

Fig. 15, N-YHS

Fig. 16, MMA

Fig. 17, HD

Fig. 18, MCNY

Fig. 19, BMFA

A flat top, without the customary pediment, is characteristic of secretaries made in New York (as of double chests and highboys made there). The example shown here, from about 1760–75 (Fig. 18), is typical in that respect, and in the stoutly modeled ball-and-claw feet with their boldly clutching knuckles. Incurved corners and carved details on the inner edge of the paneled doors add elegance to the piece. As in the case of many secretaries of the period, there are two sliding shelves at the base of the bookcase section, on which, when pulled out, candlesticks were placed.

Passing through New York on his way from Boston to Philadelphia in 1774, John Adams was impressed by the "rich" furniture he saw there. Actually, that was a strange remark for him to make, since he might have seen furniture quite as fine, although in different interpretations of the Chippendale style in and about Boston. A bombé secretary that towers to a height of more than eight feet, made around 1760 by a Bostonian named George Bright, known to his contemporaries as "the neatest workman in

Fig. 20, BMFA

town," is the most fully developed surviving example of this opulent form (Fig. 19). Its mirrored doors are framed with curved and carved gilded moldings and are flanked by pilasters in the classical Ionic style; a gilded eagle occupies a perch between the scrolls of the pediment with their pierced streamers of carved flowers and foliage—to point out but a few of this piece's distinctions. A desk, less extravagantly conceived (Fig. 20), nevertheless serves as a reminder that the bombé form was especially well understood and executed by craftsmen in the Boston area.

Boston and the surrounding area also produced block-front furniture, albeit without the distinctive shell carvings that feature the fronts of many Rhode Island case pieces. One example, a slant-front desk made in the Boston area just before the Revolutionary War, demonstrates the point (Fig. 21). Like some other desks and secretaries from this time and general area, this piece has applied half columns rising at either side from the base moldings to the pull-out rests beneath the lid.

Fig. 21, BMFA

Federal & Empire

With the passing of the Chippendale style, the slant-top desk went out of fashion, except in rural areas. The introduction of the Hepplewhite and Sheraton styles in the decades following the Revolution brought new types of writing furniture, among them the roll-top desk. The tapered, reeded legs with delicate carvings at the top associate the example illustrated (Fig. 22) with the Sheraton style and with the craftsmanship of Salem, Massachusetts. It was made about 1800–10. Roll-tops were made

Fig. 22, HFdP

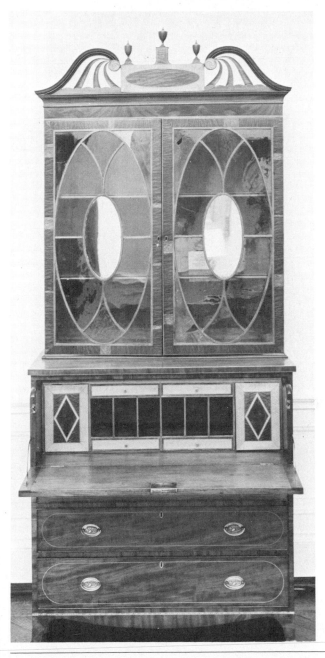

DESKS & SECRETARIES   249

elsewhere in the new nation in different interpretations of the current style. They were not common, but they serve to remind us that the golden oak roll-tops so popular with American businessmen early in our own century had distinguished antique predecessors.

Secretaries remained in fashion, but their lines took on a new lightness and grace. An example made in Baltimore in the Hepplewhite style is relieved of all carving, but its flat mahogany surfaces are enhanced by an artful use of satinwood and zebrawood

Fig. 24, HFdP

inlays (Fig. 23) in a manner characteristic of workmanship in that thriving port city.

Sheraton's *Dictionary* illustrates a number of relatively small-scaled types of writing furniture designed particularly for ladies. The piece shown in Figure 24 is modeled on what the English designer referred to as a "Lady's Cabinet and Writing Table" and was also made in Baltimore around the turn of the century. Its most distinctive feature is the use of painted and gold-leaf glass (*verre églomisé*) inserts, a practice highly developed in Baltimore. Another small desk with a compartment for books and intended for use by ladies is made in three sections, the center one in the form of a portable box with half the lid hinged to fold forward to serve as a writing surface (Fig. 25). A still smaller, compact desk consisting of a folding box with a drawer beneath mounted on reeded legs was made in Boston about 1800 (Fig. 26). As an aid to moving it about, it was equipped with a handle at either side.

Fig. 25, HFdP   Fig. 26, BMFA

An innovation of the last years of the 18th century was a compartment, fitted into a secretary-bookcase as the top central "drawer" whose face falls forward by means of a spring or quadrant to provide a writing surface, as it appears in the example here illustrated (Fig. 27). A large case piece such as this, whose center

Fig. 27, HFdP

section projects forward, we refer to as a breakfront. Sheraton called it a "Gentleman's Secretary," "intended for a gentleman to write at, keep his own accounts, and serve as a library."

An apparently unique piece, probably made in Natchez, Mississippi, about 1810–20, is a combined secretary and linen press (Fig.

Fig. 28, HPB

Fig. 29, BMFA

Fig. 30, HFdP

28). Fashioned in the Hepplewhite manner, it has graceful French feet, a shaped skirt, and, just beneath the overhanging cornice, delicately scrolled inlays.

Tambour desks, a type of furniture without any exact English prototype, were another innovation of the early years of the Republic. In these forms, popular in New England at the time, the upper case is enclosed by sliding doors, or shutters, made up of thin reeds, or slats, glued together on a canvas backing, that can be drawn out horizontally from the center (Fig. 29), or pulled up from the base in the case of roll-top desks, to reveal the interior. A number of ingenious arrangements for accommodating the writer and the draftsman, many of them the designs derived from English models, were made in America during the Federal period. As one example, a table desk fashioned in New York about 1823 in the late Sheraton style, is in fact a table, but with a reading and writing drawer supported by ratchets incorporated into one side (Fig. 30). Another piece in the same general style has a top which is hinged to fold upward to provide the writing surface beneath (Fig. 31). The twisted turnings of its legs were a common feature of American furniture in the years immediately following 1815.

Fig. 31, MCNY

Other designs in desks, or writing tables, roughly contemporary with those just mentioned, were larger in scale and were of stouter construction. George Washington reputedly used the example shown in Figure 32 during his residence in New York when that city was briefly the first capital of the United States of America in 1789–90. The ample size, large working surface, and numerous drawers, placed on all four sides, of the piece were ideally suited to the needs of a chief, or important executive; the same design was followed in other examples of the time and was copied in later years. With its boldly fluted and turned legs, another desk that could have been made for an executive is an adaptation of late Sheraton styles (Fig. 33). It was made in eastern Massachusetts about 1819.

Fig. 32, ACCNY

About the same time, Governor DeWitt Clinton of New York ordered a desk which represents the Empire style in solid, uncompromising fashion (Fig. 34). Aside from its figured mahogany veneer the essential plainness of this heavily constructed piece is relieved only by the gilded metal capitals and bases of its pilasters and those of the colonettes above the two tiers of the little interior drawers. At the other extreme of the style, a massive late Empire secretary made about 1835 by the French-born cabinetmaker Anthony Quervelle of Philadelphia is lavishly ornamented with carved elements of different varieties and an extravagantly imaginative use of matching veneers (Fig. 35). From the heavy lion-claw feet to the carved and curved, overhanging cornice, including the pointed arches and diamond shapes of the glazed doors, the

Fig. 33, HFdP

Fig. 34, MCNY

Fig. 35, MWPI

complex combination of decorative features give advance notice of the eclectic design of the Victorian period. A walnut and pine slant-top desk made in Texas about a quarter of a century later very distantly recalls the same style in an individual and very agreeably simple version (Fig. 36).

Fig. 36, HMFA

Country, School, & Office

The country artisan habitually went much his own way, adapting what current or earlier styles came to his attention in ways that fitted the needs of his customers and in terms of local woods and his own capability. Such a desk as the one here illustrated, for example (Fig. 37), made of pine and ash, can hardly be identified

Fig. 37, HFdP

with any formal style or with any specific period, although in the basic simplicity of its form (and the ingenious fitting of an extra compartment in the side of the case) it calls to mind Shaker furniture of the 19th century.

Shaker furniture was, in fact, rooted in colonial practices in workmanship and design that had been perpetuated by country craftsmen and that members of the sect brought to their own rare and severe standard of perfection. The functional character of their products is seen in a "sewing table" whose sliding shelves could be used either for sewing or writing (Fig. 38). A tall desk, or secretary, of the sort used by Shaker trustees (Fig. 39) has two lids that let down on a narrow sill separating the drawers beneath from the double storage area above.

Fig. 38, PMA

Fig. 39, HSV

DESKS & SECRETARIES 263

Fig. 40, OS

Fig. 41, WRHS

A double desk of a kind used for clerks and bookkeepers in a business office probably dates from around 1830 to 1845 (Fig. 40). The wood is painted and stained to resemble mahogany. The separate writing surfaces lift up to reveal deep storage spaces. Judging from the worn front stretcher, the piece appears to have seen long and hard use. A schoolmaster's desk, also made of painted local woods, has a similar arrangement for the storage of books and papers beneath the hinged writing surface and a spin-dled book rack for further utility (Fig. 41). The simple turning of the stout legs indicate it may have been made sometime in the middle decades of the last century. In both cases the writer obviously stood before the desk. A walnut office desk probably dating from around the Civil War period has a flat writing surface upon which are mounted two cupboards connected by a back board topped by a spindled railing (Fig. 42). The scroll-cut, incised pediments above the cupboards add an ingenuously con-ceived ornamental feature to an otherwise businesslike piece.

Fig. 42, PHS

Victorian Period

Compared to the consistently austere examples of Shaker workmanship and the more casual productions of other rural furnituremakers, desks and secretaries made in city shops during the middle decades of the 19th century were more or less elaborate creations that followed the transient modes of this early Victorian period. A walnut secretary-bookcase designed by the English-born New York architect Richard Upjohn about 1842 mingles the round arches and classical columns of Romanesque architecture with trefoils in the Gothic manner (Fig. 43). (Monumental as they often were, such forms did not always serve out their time of normal use. In one dump heap on the open prairie a group of forty-niners came across "a very handsome and new Gothic bookcase" that had been abandoned by struggling pioneers who had preceded them and which was quickly chopped up for firewood.)

A rosewood desk made in New York in the 1850s (Fig. 44) demonstrates how the rococo revival designs typical of those years were adapted to the writing needs of a fashionable lady. The slender, graceful carved cabriole legs, the scroll carvings of the pierced gallery surmounting an open shelf, and the dainty accommodation of the drawers and compartments within all marked the height of the current style. Much the same may be said of a lady's writing cabinet, also of rosewood, made in New Jersey about the same time (Fig. 45). Here the maker added a convenient shelf connecting the legs at the point of their lower, bulging curves.

Two decades later, at the other extreme from such delicate custom-made forms, the steam-powered factories of Grand Rapids and elsewhere, in the East as in the Midwest, were turning out inexpensive furniture of every description as stock-in-trade. A tall mirrored secretary with burl walnut panels and carved Corinthian applied columns (Fig. 46) is a characteristic example of the substantial mass-produced forms turned out in great quantities in the 1870s. (In 1872 it was reported that every factory in Grand Rapids had to enlarge its plant at least once every two years.)

Fig. 44, MWPI

Fig. 45, NM

Fig. 46, GRPM

Fig. 47, GRPM

In later years the term "Grand Rapids" took on some derogatory associations as standing for cheap furniture. Much of the production from that center was in fact inexpensive, but it won such a high position in the marketplace that some factories in other sections of the country used the term for their own products. The golden oak desk-bookcase shown in Figure 47, in a typical Grand Rapids style, won a prize for excellence at the Chicago World's Fair of 1893.

One of the most unusual types of desk made in the late 19th century and eagerly sought after by collectors today is the elaborate contrivance patented by W. S. Wooten of Indianapolis in 1874. When closed it resembles a massive cylinder-front desk; when opened it reveals an almost bewildering complex of pigeonholes, drawers, shelves, and other facilities (Fig. 48). It is, in fact, a veritable office complete in the one piece. Among the prominent men who owned such a remarkable (and expensive) apparatus were John D. Rockefeller, Professor Spencer F. Baird, Secretary of the Smithsonian Institution, Sidney Lanier, and Joseph Pulitzer.

Mission desks, like all the other furniture forms made in this style, which appeared at the century's close, were simple and straightforward in design and stoutly constructed of solid oak. As the style became more popular, in following decades, mass produced versions were less patiently and carefully assembled.

Fig. 48, BM

IX

Tables

Early Forms

Tables made of removable boards set on trestles were among the earliest types made in colonial America. Not many have survived. The separate top of the example illustrated (Fig. 1), made around the middle of the 17th century, is a pine board more than ten feet long. It sits on oak trestles joined by a long brace held in place by wooden pegs. The piece could be easily disassembled and the parts put aside to make room for other household functions. Space-saving features were built into early folding, or gateleg, tables, a type of furniture that became popular in England in the early 1600s. A colonial example made around 1680 has a fixed top supported by stoutly turned legs that rise from trestle bases. Two hinged leaves can be raised to rest on gates that swing out from the central structure for support (Fig. 2).

For good reason, tables of this general functional character, following the fashions of successive periods, have been made ever since, as will be seen. Butterfly tables, so named because of the wing shape of the brackets that support the hinged leaves, are apparently a distinctive early American variant of the form (Fig. 3). The brackets that serve instead of gates swivel on the side stretchers, which are sometimes handsomely turned like the raking legs. Tops are usually but not always oval or circular when the leaves are extended. Quality in these pieces is judged by the shape

Fig. 1, MMA

Fig. 2, HFM

Fig. 3, BG

of the wings, the character of the turnings, and the rake of the legs.

What are today called stretcher tables were typical Jacobean forms of the 17th century. Obviously they are so labeled because of the prominent heavy stretchers that bind together the four legs. The latter are often boldly turned in the spirit of the great chairs and cupboards of the times. One example, its feet worn away after centuries of use, has relatively simple baluster-shaped legs and a drawer with lightly carved intersecting semicircles, or lunettes (Fig. 4). The overhanging top is of pine, the rest of the table oak. Such a piece, a form of center table, may be considered the ancestor of later library and parlor tables. The legs of another example of these bulky joined forms are turned in a robust, bulbous

Fig. 4, SI

pattern (Fig. 5). Possibly to facilitate moving, its top is detachable. In place, it overhangs a molded apron with a scrolled and bracketed skirting with turned pendants. The "bun" feet are a type often found on 17th-century furniture.

Toward the close of the century and with the advent of the William and Mary period, new varieties of smaller tables were introduced. The butterfly table, already described, was one example. Tavern tables, low, sturdy, and rectangular, sometimes with a drawer, and with turned stretchers and legs, developed out of Jacobean origins to become widely popular in the 1700s (Fig. 6). Although they also served for domestic uses, these lighter, easily movable forms could be conveniently placed before a visitor in an inn or tavern, by which token they acquired the name given to them

Fig. 5, WA

Fig. 6, WA

Fig. 7, MMA   Fig. 8, WA

in modern times. What for evident reason are called splay-leg tables enjoyed favor around the turn of the century. A fair example of this type, from about 1710, has turned legs raking in four directions and terminating in Spanish feet, molded stretchers, a shaped skirt, and an oval top (Fig. 7). Tables of this kind, apparently a peculiarly American development, were made of various woods (walnut in the present case) and sometimes painted. Except for the solid top they closely resembled the more convenient and flexible butterfly tables that succeeded them. One ingenious type of space-saver known as a tuck-away table has a single gate with notches at the top of its posts. The posts when folded into the notches made to receive them permit the entire top to drop flat against the uprights to permit easy storage of the piece (Fig. 8).

Reflecting a growing interest in more spacious living, large gate-leg tables were designed principally, if not exclusively, as dining tables for rooms set aside for meals. To support larger and heavier leaves, many of such tables were equipped with double sets of swinging gates. The very impressive example here illustrated (Fig. 9), made of mahogany about 1700 in Albany, New York, extends to almost six feet in diameter, with twelve identically shaped upright members.

Fig. 9, AIHA

Colonial 18th-Century

Another indication of new living styles comes with the introduction of the dressing table in the William and Mary period. This was a specialized form that had no precedent in the 17th century. In its general style it also marked a distinct break with Jacobean traditions. A more or less typical specimen dating from the first decades of the 18th century (Fig. 10) is made of walnut with cup-turned legs joined by crisscrossing flat stretchers. From a shaped skirt opening into an arch at the center two pendants complement the finial at the crossing of the stretchers. A shallow drawer above the arch is flanked by a deeper drawer on each side, presumably for brushes, combs, and similar paraphernalia; all these drawers are surrounded by thin rounded moldings. Not infrequently, as in the case of other pieces of this time and style, the flat surfaces of such tables are covered with decorative veneers.

Fig. 10, WA

Another dressing table, made of cherry in Connecticut about 1740–60 (Fig. 11), exemplifies the simplification of furniture designs that came about with the advent of the Queen Anne style. The relative severity of the frame of the piece is relieved by the handsomely scalloped top and the curving design of the skirt. Slender cabriole legs terminate in pad feet resting on "cushions"; the elaborate stretchers of the William and Mary style have been altogether dispensed with.

So it was with other types of tables of the Queen Anne period. The rather complicated earlier forms of dining tables, with their gates of turned uprights and stretchers, gave way to simpler designs and arrangements, better referred to now as drop-leaf tables. When raised into position, two simply shaped leaves, rounded or rectangular, were each supported by one of the cabriole legs, which was hinged to swing out from the central section (Fig. 12).

During the Queen Anne period tea and coffee, virtually unknown in the colonies in the previous century, had become popular, and special tables, smaller than dining tables, were designed for conveniently serving those beverages. The different

Fig. 11, HFdP

Fig. 12, HFM

Fig. 13, HFdP

forms such conveniences might take is suggested by two contrasting examples, both from about 1725–40. One, with its dished top, shallow, lightly accented apron, slender cabriole legs, and pad feet is a characteristic sophisticated New England piece of the period (Fig. 13); the other also has a dished top, but it otherwise expressed the Queen Anne style in the simplest provincial terms (Fig. 14). Its boldly raked legs would provide some additional stability were the floor uneven.

Another, distinctive type that developed during this period—one that guaranteed even greater stability—was the tripod table, a form that gained in popularity as the century advanced. Such handy tables commonly had tops that could be tilted when the piece was not in use, as in the painted example shown here from mid-century (Fig. 15). Other tables of modest size were made for occasional use. One type with rounded extensions at the four corners of the top (Fig. 16) is variously termed a porringer or a breakfast table, although obviously it could be used for a variety of purposes.

Fig. 14, HFdP

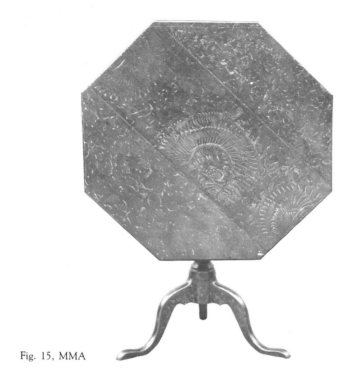

Fig. 15, MMA

Fig. 16, HFdP

Many types of tables made in the Chippendale style are basically similar to those developed in the Queen Anne period, but are often more richly carved. The cabriole leg remained in favor, however, in these later years, commonly terminating in a ball-and-claw foot. Those points are clearly evident in a mahogany dressing table (Fig. 17) made in Philadelphia about 1760–70. In later years this form became known as a lowboy, since it was now more commonly made as a companion piece to what is called a highboy. Similar carved elaboration is the only essential difference between the fine tripod tilt-top tables of the Chippendale period (Fig. 18) and early examples of this form. The more highly developed Chippendale examples are equipped with a "bird cage," a device set between the top and the supporting shaft that permits the top both to tilt and to rotate (Fig. 19).

Gate-leg, or drop leaf, dining tables continued to be made in the same general fashion as Queen Anne types, except again for carvings and ball-and-claw feet, although in England they were becoming outmoded. A singular, small variant of such folding tables was the spider-leg table, rectangular in form and fragile in appearance and so named because of its extremely slender turned legs and stretchers (Fig. 20). Another kind of small folding table,

Fig. 17, BMFA

Fig. 18, MMA

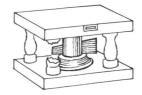

Fig. 19

Fig. 20, AIHA

often used for breakfasting and known as a "Pembroke," was designed during the Chippendale period with two narrow leaves or flaps which when extended were supported not by a gate or swinging legs but by hinged wooden brackets. Typically, they had straight legs and crossed stretchers, as in the example made some time during the Revolutionary War period shown here (Fig. 21). As will be seen, the Pembroke became an extremely popular form in different styles in years to come.

The growing popularity of cards and other games called for tables especially designed to accommodate the needs of the players, with folding tops that could be laid back on a supporting hinged leg to enlarge the gaming surface and with square depressions at the four corners for candlesticks and oval "fishponds" to hold such counters as may have been used in the play. As in the example illustrated here (Fig. 22), such gaming tables sometimes

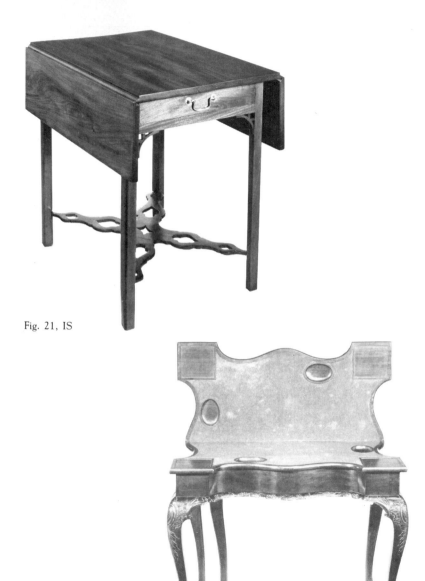

Fig. 21, IS

Fig. 22, IS

included a fifth leg as the supporting member for the top when it was folded back ready for the game. In less elaborate models one of just two rear legs swings outward for support of a relatively simple folding top.

In the decades on either side of the Revolutionary War, Philadelphia was the leading metropolis of America and one of the largest cities in the British empire. While its craftsmen were developing highly sophisticated versions of the Chippendale style, the Germans who had settled in the nearby countryside continued to make furniture that clung tenaciously to old traditions. The medieval heritage is clearly evident in a sawbuck table from about 1750 with its X-shaped supports (Fig. 23), a form derived from Gothic patterns of northern Europe. (Such tables are still being produced for use in the country.) Another table with turned legs, heavy stretchers, a removable top, and a heart motif pierced in the naively scrolled apron (Fig. 24) is a variant of a type long since outmoded in urban centers. So also is a painted pine table with turned, raking legs joined by stretchers (Fig. 25).

An early kind of settee with a back folding down on the arms to serve as a table top and with a storage space beneath the hinged seat is known in this country as a hutch table (Fig. 26). It is obviously closely related to the 17th-century chair-tables already described (see pages 64–66). Country-made versions of this serviceable form were produced into the 19th century.

Fig. 23, PMA

Fig. 24, PMA

Fig. 25, PMA

Fig. 26, BM

Post-Revolutionary

Following the Revolutionary War, during the long period in which classical revival styles held sway, old forms of tables took on different guises and some altogether new forms were developed. Pembroke tables gained in popularity and were made in considerable quantity with local and regional variations in the details of their design. An example made of mahogany in Baltimore around the turn of the century (Fig. 27) has tapered legs, square in section, typical of the patterns illustrated in Hepplewhite's *Guide*. Like many others of this general type, it is ornamented with delicate inlays of lighter wood. The flaps, or leaves, are gracefully shaped. In other cases these may be simply rounded or rectangular, and the legs may be round and reeded in the Sheraton manner. Pembrokes often included a drawer at one end, as in the case of a brightly painted provincial example (Fig. 28), made in later years and demonstrating the individual character these forms could take.

Tables with folding tops—almost always referred to as card tables, although if they had no indentations for chips or counters, as they often did not, they were undoubtedly used for various purposes—also rose in popularity with the new styles. (They were sometimes made in pairs.) In these, as in other American forms designed in the late 18th and early 19th centuries, features derived from the books of both Hepplewhite and Sheraton were combined in a single piece. Figure 29 illustrates one such table, with its tapering legs of square section as favored by Hepplewhite and its top with rounded or D-shaped corners familiar in Sheraton patterns. Another roughly contemporary example (Fig. 30) has round, reeded, tapering legs in the Sheraton style. Both are inlaid and, while in general they are highly typical of American workmanship of the time, they particularly represent types of such tables made in New England.

A type of card table, based on Sheraton and introduced by the notable New York furnituremaker Duncan Phyfe, has three in-

Fig. 27, BMFA

Fig. 28, S

Fig. 29, BMFA

Fig. 30, BMFA

curved legs supporting a vase-shaped pedestal, all carved with an acanthus leaf design (Fig. 31), and with a cloverleaf top (Fig. 32). (Some years after Phyfe's death, another New York furnituremaker wrote that Phyfe's chief merit was in "Especially improving of the 'Sheraton' style.") Although this graceful form is usually identified with Phyfe, other known contemporary New York craftsmen produced pieces that are all but identical with those bearing Phyfe's label. Lyre-shaped and columned supports resting on a platform often replaced the central pedestal in card

Fig. 31

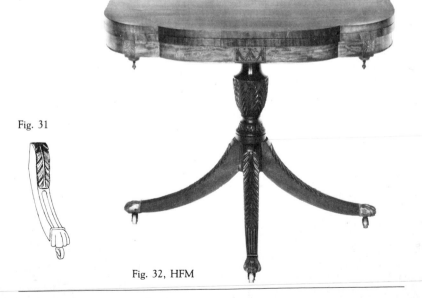

Fig. 32, HFM

tables of the Empire period (Fig. 33). An elaborately carved and gilded card table made by the French émigré craftsman Charles Honoré Lannuier of New York is very close in spirit to French inventions of the Napoleonic period (Fig. 34). The bird-headed and winged curving front supports, the applied metal mounts on the base, and the lion-paw feet with their leafy appendages show America's version of the Empire style in its most sophisticated form. The heavily scrolled feet and the boldly stenciled skirt of another example from about 1825–30 (Fig. 35) are

Fig. 33, BMFA

Fig. 34, HFM

Fig. 35, MMA

characteristic of the late phase of the Empire style, harbingers of the dawning Victorian era.

Sewing tables were a new form introduced into America from England late in the 18th century. In 1803, Sheraton described the type as a "Table with a Bag, used by the Ladies to work at, in which they deposit their fancy needlework"—a description which fits a typical, fine example probably made in Boston about the time

Fig. 36, HFdP

Sheraton published his statement (Fig. 36). Like others produced in New England at approximately the same time, this piece has a square top with canted corners and two small drawers. The bag was accessible when the lower drawer was opened. It is made of mahogany with figured veneers of light-colored woods. The massive solidity of another example from around 1825 (Fig. 37) is a symptom of the decline of the classical revival style in the late

Fig. 37, NM

Empire period. However, with its relatively large lion-paw feet and the gilt stenciling that decorates the stocky pillars, the design has merits that still appeal, as they must have when the piece was produced.

In sewing stands as well as every other furniture form the Shakers produced their own versions in which "style" is reduced to the simplest practical design. The example illustrated (Fig. 38) has drawers that slide on cleats and that can be pulled from either side, which permitted two women sitting on either side to cooperate on the task in hand.

The pier table was another form that was introduced into America with the classical revival period and that enjoyed long

Fig. 38, HFdP

popularity. It was a kind of side table, somewhat higher than average, designed to stand against a pier, a section of wall between two windows or doors, and was often surmounted by what was called a pier glass (see page 393). The earliest American-made examples followed the same general patterns as card tables in the Hepplewhite and Sheraton styles. (Quite probably card tables often were used instead of pier tables.)

Late Empire examples of the 1830s took on a separate character, with ponderous supports and mirrored backs. As in the case of some earlier side tables, they have marble tops, indicating that they too were sometimes used as mixing tables (Fig. 39). In the ultimate phase of the classical revival rich carving and gilded

Fig. 39, IMA

decoration gave way to flat, often veneered, surfaces of mahogany or rosewood with bold, machine-sawed, scrolled supports and feet (Fig. 36 in Historical Introduction). A mahogany card table (Fig. 40) also exemplifies this boldly simplified style, which remained in vogue for decades. (In 1833, one New York furnituremaker advertised just such a piece at fifty dollars. He died a very rich man.)

Fig. 40, N-YHS

Later 19th-Century

The medley of different styles that superseded the classical revival in the middle decades of the 19th century brought forth a wide variety of tables, as of other forms of furniture. Most of them served old, familiar functions but in different dress, so to speak. As earlier observed, the furniture that was thought best to express the Gothic spirit was largely produced under the direction of architects to complement their Gothic revival buildings. In short, they were usually custom made. Such was an octagonal table with cusped arches connecting its stout octagonal uprights (Fig. 41) designed by Alexander Jackson Davis for one of his "baronial castles."

Also as remarked earlier, the slightest detail suggesting Gothic motifs seems sufficient to relate a piece to this style. The crocketed

Fig. 41, L

ornament carved at the base of the columns of a sofa table made in Baltimore in the 1850s (Fig. 42) serves the purpose, although the piece is essentially a late Sheraton form. As Sheraton pointed out, this type of table was intended to be "used before a sofa" by ladies engaged in reading, writing, or needlework. With their flaps or brackets at either end such forms represent an enlarged, elongated kind of Pembroke table.

At about the same time, the 1850s, Joseph Henry Belter produced the intricately carved rosewood center table with marble top shown in Figure 43, a piece that summarizes the characteristics of the Victorian rococo-revival style usually associated with his name, as described in the Introduction. The table is one of a group of other furniture forms that were designed *en suite* for a room in a New York dwelling. One of Belter's contemporaries produced a card table, shaped in rococo curves, that is a somewhat less exuberant expression of the same general style (Fig. 44). As in earlier, classical revival examples, the rear legs pivot outward to support the folding top. In extreme contrast to such highly modish specimens, a simple, ball- or spool-turned occasional table represents a style of furniture that was widely popular at roughly the same time (Fig. 45). Factory-made, mass-produced, and inexpen-

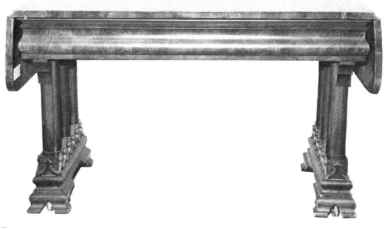

Fig. 42, BMA

Fig. 43, MCNY

Fig. 44, MWPI

sive, such forms were used in less formal interiors and classified as cottage furniture.

With the approach of the Civil War, tables of various types made in what was vaguely termed the Renaissance-revival style became highly fashionable and remained so into the last quarter of the century. As in the case of other forms in this composite style, the naturalistic carved ornament of the rococo style was replaced by more geometric designs. A marble-topped table made of walnut about 1860 represents a transitional phase of this style (Fig. 46). Scroll curves are still retained but they are imbedded in a heavier structure of other elements bearing no relation to the rococo. As the style advanced, carving gave way to flat surfaces with decorations typically outlined by incised lines, often gilded, and surrounding inset panels of burl or to inlaid designs of different colored woods as seen in a sewing table (Fig. 47) and a parlor table

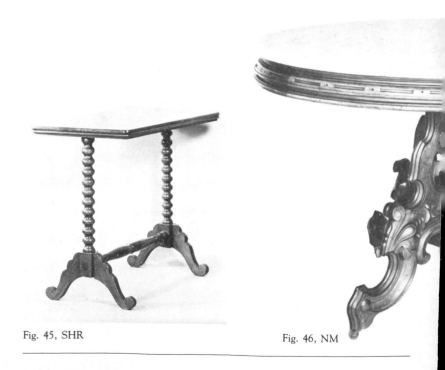

Fig. 45, SHR   Fig. 46, NM

(Fig. 48), both dating from about 1870. The legs or central pedestals of tables in this style frequently take the shape of a Renaissance vase or urn (Fig. 49). Machine production played an important role in the character of these pieces, particularly demonstrated by the simple, flat elements that compose the sewing table.

Between the Centennial Exposition of 1876 and the Columbian Exposition of 1893, tables were introduced that markedly contrasted with models in the Renaissance-revival style. Far lighter in construction and with more delicate inlays of richly contrasting materials, they are fairly represented by an example with saber-shaped legs tapering to slender brass ferrules and a marble top with a rosewood border inlaid with mother-of-pearl (Fig. 50). Another rosewood table, also with mother-of-pearl inlays, with additional gilt decoration, and, again with saberlike

Fig. 47, GRPM

Fig. 48, NM

Fig. 49

Fig. 50, MCNY

feet, shows the same general style in a variant form (Fig. 51).
During these years, Oriental influences were apparent in many of
these occidental forms, as in a side table with three latticework
panels suggesting Japanese designs (Fig. 52).

This was the day of Turkish cozy-corners, no one of which could
be considered complete without an inlaid Damascus table similar
to the one here illustrated (Fig. 53). It was also a period in which

Fig. 51, MCNY

Fig. 52, L

Fig. 53, SI

Fig. 54, MMA

Fig. 55, SH

bamboo furniture was imported from China and Japan which had the merit of being "strongly made and easily kept clean." Naturalized versions of these exotic pieces were made in America of maple lathe-turned to simulate bamboo (Fig. 54). They were often designed in sets of various forms for bedrooms.

A variety of tables of more indigenous and more or less nondescript design were being produced during the last years of the century in factories across the land. One Grand Rapids firm advertised a table identical with the one here illustrated (Fig. 55) as "our leader," priced according to size, from eighty-five cents to one dollar seventy-five; brass feet cost an additional fifty cents. At the opposite extreme, it was at this time that Gustave Stickley was introducing his heavy solid oak "Craftsman" furniture, to become known as Mission furniture (Fig. 56).

Fig. 56, MMA

X

Daybeds, Settees, & Sofas

L
ate in the 17th century special forms designed for repose during the day were introduced into colonial America. Day-beds, or couches, were actually extensions of contemporary chairs (what the French called *chaises longues,* or long chairs) and developed in the same styles. An example from the William and Mary period exhibits the reverse-scroll, or Flemish scroll carvings (Fig. 1) and the caning characteristic of that time (Fig. 2). Such pieces were usually provided with cushions and had canted backs for added comfort. The back of a walnut daybed made in Pennsylvania probably in the second quarter of the 18th century is fitted with chains so that it can be raised or lowered as desired (Fig. 3); legs and posts are stoutly turned.

The daybed continued to be an important item of household furnishing until the middle years of the 18th century. Figure 4 represents an exceptionally handsome example in the Queen Anne style made of walnut in Philadelphia around 1740–50. The carved cresting, the scrolled back splats, the cabriole legs, and the trifid feet are comparable to the corresponding features of chairs made then and there.

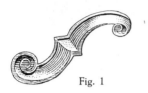

Fig. 1

Fig. 2, MMA

Fig. 3, HFM

As the century progressed, settees and sofas gradually assumed an important place in the fully equipped colonial houses, and the daybed vanished. The tall, shaped back and the horizontally rolled arms of a settee made in Philadelphia about 1735 recall easy-chair designs of a generation earlier; but the shell-carved cabriole legs with trifid feet are in the local Queen Anne style (Fig. 5). The sofa came to maturity, it might be said, in the Chippendale period. Typical aspects of this development are represented by the two examples shown here. Both have serpentine-shaped backs. In one case the arms are vertically rolled like those of the easy chairs in the Chippendale style, the legs are cabriole with ball-and-claw feet (Fig. 6); in the other, tapering legs with spade feet (Fig. 7) herald the influence of Hepplewhite's designs (Fig. 8).

During the first decades of the 19th century the sofa became an increasingly common furniture form. The pattern books of the period illustrated a wide variety of designs for this form. An example made in Salem about 1800 and probably carved by the master craftsman Samuel McIntyre, is almost a literal reproduction of one of Sheraton's designs (Fig. 9). Because of its light, attractive appearance, caning, so popular in the late 17th century, was revived at the end of the 18th. The reeding of both the horizontal and the vertical elements of a caned mahogany sofa, as well as the carving on the back rail, are characteristic of work

Fig. 5, MMA

Fig. 6, MMA

Fig. 7

Fig. 8, HFM

Fig. 9, MMA

Fig. 10, HFdP

Fig. 11, HFM

produced by Duncan Phyfe of New York early in the century (Fig. 10). The subtle curve of the arms as they arch down to join the upright posts is also typical of his refined craftsmanship. A couch, probably also made by Duncan Phyfe about 1820–30, corresponds to what Sheraton termed a "Grecian squab" (Fig. 11). Its Empire design was derived from that of the banqueting couches used by ancient Romans. Because the famous artist of Napoleon's France, Jacques Louis David, painted the beautiful Madame Récamier reclining on such a piece, this general type of sofa is commonly known as a récamier.

Variously labeled a love seat, a tête-à-tête, or a conversational, the seating arrangement illustrated in Figure 12 is in the rococo-revival style of John Henry Belter. Like his other furniture forms,

it is made of laminated and shaped rosewood with the addition of complex carved ornament. The prominent 19th-century American landscape architect Andrew Jackson Downing explained that with such a convenience a wife could sit toward the light of a lamp as she sewed, while her husband sat reading his book by the light of a fire.

A spindled settee made in the 1850s at the Shaker community at Enfield, New Hampshire, stands in sharp contrast to the highly decorated, fashionable furniture of the time (Fig. 13). According to a visitor to one of the Shaker communities, these people believed that their furniture was "originally designed in heaven, and that the patterns have been transmitted to them by angels."

Also around the middle of the century, another unsung

Fig. 13, PMA

Fig. 14, SIDC

craftsman from the Swedish Jansenite community at Bishop Hill, Illinois, constructed a spindled pew for the local church (Fig. 14). In this simple piece there is no pretension to formal style. In 1876 advertisements pictured sofas identical with the one shown in Figure 15 as part of a "Solid Walnut Parlor suit" consisting of seven pieces covered in horsehair, all for the price of $65 (see Fig. 106, Chapter II). On receipt of the price mentioned, such suites would be "packed and shipped to any part of the world." This modified version of the rococo-revival style was understandably extremely popular in the 1860s and 1870s.

In the Empire period and years to follow, the French termed a sofa with one end higher than the other a *méridienne*. An American version made of flat-sawn, incised members was mass-produced in the 1870s (Fig. 16), to satisfy a growing public

Fig. 15, HFM

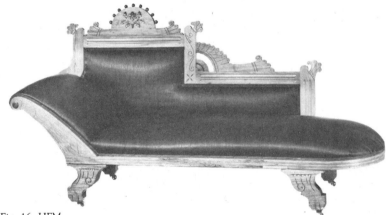

Fig. 16, HFM

demand for "fashionable" household gear and for previously unexperienced "comforts" at a price it could afford.

Following the Civil War improved textile manufacturing, increasing use of sewing machines, and the perfecting of spiral metal springs gave upholsterers unprecedented opportunities to practice and expand their trade. For soft seating furniture, as in the case of a love seat of the 1880s (Fig. 17), upholstery often completely concealed the structural framework of a piece.

With furniture in the Mission style, characteristically sworn to structural honesty openly arrived at, no such deep comforts were indulged. An oak sofa made in that popular style around the turn of the century, with its solid, exposed framework offers little inducement to lolling or lounging (Fig. 18).

Fig. 17, MCNY

Fig. 18, HFM

XI

Dining Furniture

As a separate room with specialized furnishings the dining room was a rare feature of American homes until after the Revolution. Earlier in the 18th century, for instance, the Samuel Sewalls of Boston entertained nine quests for dinner in Mr. Sewall's bed chamber, probably eating from a gate-leg table with the leaves raised.

A development of the next century was the sectional dining table. An example made in Baltimore about 1800–10 in the Hepplewhite style is composed of two semicircular sections with drop leaves that, when raised and joined together, brought the piece to its full usable length (Fig. 1). (Sometimes the leaves were attached to a central, third section, freeing the semicircular ends for use as side tables when the full length of all the parts put together was not needed.) A large banquet board in three divisions, with its four-column platformed supports and its gracefully outsweeping legs, is an impressive example of a typically New York style of the early 19th century associated with the work of Duncan Phyfe (Fig. 2). Brass clips join the sections together.

In other examples the central pedestal was surmounted by an accordionlike device on which, when extended, additional leaves of varying number could be laid (Fig. 3). Roughly similar arrangements for increasing the length of the table top have been employed ever since. Thus the pedestal of the heavy Gothic-style

Fig. 1, IS

Fig. 3, IS

Fig. 2, MMA

dining table shown in Figure 4 is designed in two sections which when drawn apart provide space for extra leaves to be dropped into place.

The sideboard was an important innovation of the classical revival period. An inlaid mahogany example in the Hepplewhite

Fig. 4, MWPI

style, typical of many produced in the New York–New Jersey area, has a serpentine front with a recessed section under the central drawer (Fig. 5). The flanking cupboards are incurved. It was probably made in New Jersey about 1785. A kidney-shaped example in the Sheraton style was made in Philadelphia about 1800 and

Fig. 5, BMFA

bears the label of the maker, Henry Connelly (Fig. 6). (Some English sideboards, and possibly some American ones, were supplied with a small cupboard to contain a chamber pot for the immediate relief of those who drank too much during the course of a long meal.)

A semi-elliptical sideboard with four "French feet," made in Salem, Massachusetts, around 1800, is a variant of the more usual form (Fig. 7). A comparable form is illustrated in Hepplewhite's *Guide*. The keyholes on all these examples indicate that the silverware, wines, and other adjuncts to dining that were kept in these pieces were securely locked up when they were not in active use. Separate cases, also equipped with lock and key, were often designed to hold silver tableware and were usually placed on sideboards. One of three made in New York and resembling several illustrated in Sheraton's *Drawing Book* has elaborate silver mounts in the Chippendale style (Fig. 8). Curiously, they date from about 1770, a number of years before Sheraton's publication appeared. Another example of different design is made of contrast-

Fig. 6, PMA

ing veneers and inlays and is mounted on a pedestal (Fig. 9). According to Sheraton, such pieces were the work of specialists and were not made in regular cabinet shops.

A sideboard with tapered reeded legs in the Sheraton manner

Fig. 7, BMFA

Fig. 8, MMA

Fig. 9, BG

Fig. 10, BMFA

Fig. 11, BMFA

Fig. 12, CW

Fig. 13, HFdP

and a top in two tiers has a front designed with concave curves in the middle section (Fig. 10). This hollowed arrangement, Sheraton averred, "will sometimes secure the butler from the jostles of the other servants." The piece illustrated here was probably made in Boston about 1800–10 and retains what are apparently its original glass knobs. A much smaller version—it might be called a sideboard-table—was probably designed to stand between two windows (Fig. 11). That convenient scale was apparently especially favored in New England.

Although they were made in all parts of the country, cellarets, designed for the locked storage of wines and spirits, were more popular in the southern states than elsewhere. An early example is raised on a small stand with a drawer and with cabriole legs and slipper feet in the Queen Anne style (Fig. 12). The broad and clearly revealed dovetailing of the case itself suggests an early date,

Fig. 14, HFdP

Fig. 15, BMFA

although the brasses are typical of the Chippendale period. Another example, from around 1800, has splayed legs, square-sectioned and tapered in the Hepplewhite manner (Fig. 13). Both pieces were made of walnut somewhere in the South and their interiors are divided into compartments to hold bottles.

Wine coolers were also more common in the South than elsewhere. They normally were placed under sideboards, as were cellarets when they were without stands. An oval, lidded example, possibly made in Charleston, South Carolina, very late in the 18th century, was apparently intended to serve as a cellarette as well (Fig. 14). The cistern of a Boston cooler made about the same time is composed of vertical bands of alternating mahogany and satinwood veneers bound with two brass hoops and standing on four turned, reeded, and carved legs (Fig. 15). The well is partly lined with sheet lead. Two lion-mask and ring handles of gilded

Fig. 16, HFdP

brass add to the elegance of this outstanding example. Generally speaking it need hardly be added, such forms were commissioned only by those who could afford the good life.

Tea was also customarily kept under lock and key, in small chests that were often divided into three interior compartments shaped to hold rectangular canisters for as many different kinds of tea. The example illustrated (Fig. 16) with its delicate inlays and its ivory keyhole plate represents in miniature scale the elegance of the federal style of the early 1800s.

The hunt board, even more distinctly a southern type of furniture, is essentially a modified form of sideboard. Since it was principally used as a serving table for the food and drink provided for hunters standing about before and after the chase, it is simpler and sometimes higher than the sideboard (Fig. 17).

Among other specialized forms that gained popularity in post-Revolutionary America were mixing tables, adjuncts to hospitality, usually with marble tops or surfaces that alcohol would not stain. (Thomas Jefferson referred to one at the White House in

Fig. 17, FAMS

1809 as "an elegant Mahogany *drink Table* with a Marble Top.") A small, relatively simple example in the Hepplewhite style (Fig. 18) may have been used beside the chair of a seated drinker. A more elaborate piece made in Baltimore has a tamboured top that rolls down to conceal the interior and two flanking drawers for decanters (Fig. 19).

Another marble-topped table, smaller in scale and earlier in date (about 1760–90), was probably designed as a tea-kettle stand, although it may have doubled for a mixing table (Fig. 20). For further utility it has a storage space beneath the top, a drawer, and a pull-out shelf to hold a cup or glass while it was being filled.

The early 19th-century dumbwaiter shown in Figure 21 is an interesting rarity among early American furnishings. Such devices were, as Sheraton noted in his *Dictionary*, "intended for the use of the dining parlour, on which to place glasses of wine, and plates, both clean and such as have been used." The shelves revolve as a single unit to facilitate this procedure.

Sideboards kept pace with the changing styles as the 19th

Fig. 18, HFdP

Fig. 19, MMA

Fig. 20, HFdP

Fig. 21, HFdP

century advanced. An example made in New York about 1815, possibly by the French-born cabinetmaker Charles Honoré Lannuier, displays the large, plain surfaces, the engaged classical columns, the lion's-paw feet, and the lion's-head brasses that are all characteristic of the Empire style (Fig. 22). Tambour shutters close before the center section and curved pineapple finials accent the back board. Another sideboard, made about 1825–35, with its stencilled gilding, applied metal ornaments, and huge carved winged feet, epitomizes the later Empire style in this form (Fig. 23). An oak serving board of the late 19th century (Fig. 24) speaks as emphatically for the machine-made versions so typical of that period. In its flat surfaces and simple outlines, a sideboard turned out at about the same time shows even more clearly the ways in which designs were adapted to the possibilities and the limitations of the machine (Fig. 25).

Fig. 22, HFM

Fig. 23, HMFA

Fig. 24, NM

Fig. 25, HFM

XII

Beds & Cradles

F ew, if any, American beds have survived from the 17th century, but for some reason a number of cradles have. An elaborate example that descended in the family of a Mayflower passenger has a hood of turned spindles capped by a solid "roof" at the head of the piece (Fig. 1). The body of the cradle is made up of pine panels within a molded oak frame; the four corner posts are spliced over solid rockers. Rounded knobs on the front two posts provided a convenient grip for whoever rocked the infant. Another paneled example made of walnut in the Hudson River Valley with an open hood and the date 1673 carved on the headboard has turned knobs on the sides for securing an outer coverlet (Fig. 2), as does a somewhat simpler cradle the bottom of which is made of ropes stretched across the base of the frame in the manner of early bedsteads (Fig. 3). A bed wrench (Fig. 4) was used to tighten the ropes when they sagged.

Provision for such roping can be seen in an early low-post bedstead, and the actual roping in place in its attendant trundle, or truckle, bed (Fig. 5). The latter, as was often the case, is fitted with wheels so that, when not in use, it could easily be rolled out of the way under the "parent" bedstead. Trundles were customarily used by children (over cradle age) and servants.

It is well to recall here that the word "bed" as it was customarily

Fig. 1, WA

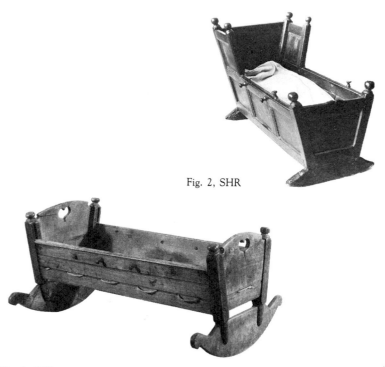

Fig. 2, SHR

Fig. 3, CW

Fig. 4, CW

Fig. 5, IS

used in early colonial America referred to what we now term bedding; thus, records from that period mention feather beds, down beds, etc. The wooden frame on which these materials were laid was known as a *bedstead*. Among the oldest such frames that have survived are a number that were designed to fold up against a wall when not in use, such as the early 18th-century example illustrated in Figures 6 and 7.

There are probably no extant specimens of four-poster American beds earlier than the Queen Anne period, and even from then they are very rare. The example shown here (Fig. 8) has the cabriole legs with pad feet so typical of the Queen Anne style and round, tapered posts supporting its crewelwork hangings of the mid-18th century. For the better part of a century to come the

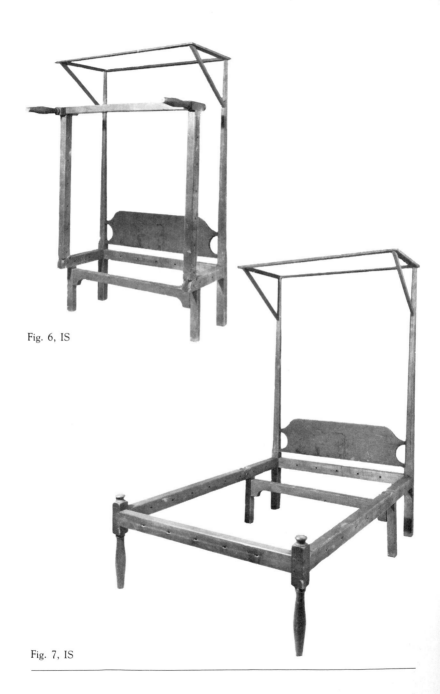

Fig. 6, IS

Fig. 7, IS

Fig. 8, HFdP

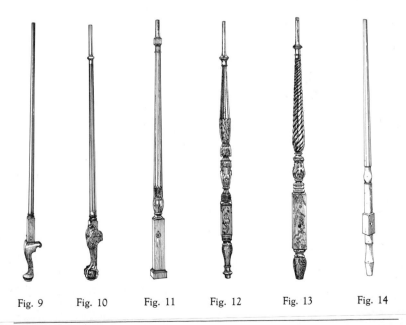

Fig. 9   Fig. 10   Fig. 11   Fig. 12   Fig. 13   Fig. 14

four-poster remained in vogue, the most significant variations being in the design of the posts, which for the most part followed the furniture styles of the successive periods as indicated in the accompanying drawings (Fig. 9, Queen Anne; Fig 10, Chippendale; Fig. 11, late 18th century; Fig. 12, Sheraton; Fig. 13, 1825–40). One type of no particular formal style is slim, tapered, and shaped with six or eight sides, like a pencil (Fig. 14). It is believed that most pencil-post beds date from before the Revolution. In another type of bed of light proportions, known as a field bed, the posts support an arched overhead frame (Fig. 15). Sometimes also referred to as tent beds, these forms were adapted from the folding, portable beds used in the field during military campaigns. Although they were made much earlier, they were particularly fashionable in the post-Revolutionary War decades and commonly followed designs published by Sheraton and Hepplewhite.

In passing, the Windsor principle was applied to cradle design. An example made in Boston late in the 18th century has spindles turned to simulate the natural design of bamboo (Fig. 16).

Fig. 15, IS

Around the second decade of the 19th century a type of bed with curved panel ends became extremely popular. Today we refer to them as Empire or sleigh beds; they were earlier advertised as French or Grecian beds. They were intended to stand with the side, rather than the head, to the wall, sometimes in alcoves. Although superb examples were made, such as that by Charles Honoré Lannuier, with its applied gilt-bronze ornaments and its satinwood veneer panels (Fig. 17), others of less pretension were made in quantities. One such, simply painted, shows how the style was adapted for modest service as a form of cottage furniture (Fig. 18). Still others were cast in iron when the use of that metal became a popular novelty in house and garden furnishings. Around the middle of the century low beds with spool turnings, so-called Jenny Lind beds, were manufactured in large quantities. Because they were of light construction and inexpensive, they enjoyed great popularity, and they are still in demand today.

Stylish beds of the later 19th century often assumed massive dimensions and dispensed with the four posts in favor of more elaborate head- and footboards. An impressive example, stamped

Fig. 16, BG

Fig. 17, AIHA

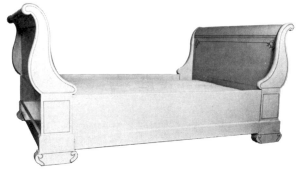

Fig. 18, SHR

Fig. 19, BM

with the name of John Henry Belter and made around 1860, magnificently displays that craftsman's technique of steam-pressing and molding laminated layers of wood in its broad, unbroken expanses of carved rosewood veneer crested with luxuriantly carved ornament (Fig. 19). An oak bed made for Lyndhurst in Tarrytown, New York, possibly designed by Alexander Jackson Davis, architect of that remarkable building, is one of the most successful realizations of the Gothic revival style in furniture (Fig. 20). Lyndhurst was built in the 1840s. With its monumental, crested pediment and lavishly carved and turned ornament, a walnut and burl bedstead turned out at Grand Rapids about 1875 in what was termed the Renaissance style is almost overpowering in its sheer bulk (Fig. 21). Another typical Grand

Fig. 20, L

Rapids product of the 1870s reduces the same general formula to its simplest machine-made terms (Fig. 22).

In contrast to such stylish and often elaborate construction the Shakers fashioned beds of a timeless simplicity (Fig. 23), this one from about 1800–30. Like the earlier trundle beds, their legs terminated in rollers, not to move them under other beds, but to facilitate housekeeping.

As the century dwindled and styles changed, beds in the

Fig. 21, TRB

Fig. 22, HFM

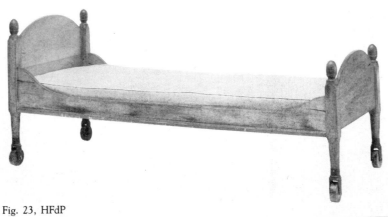

Fig. 23, HFdP

Eastlake manner had their vogue, relying on straightforward construction, natural wood finishes, and the inevitable spindle ornament. In the example illustrated (Fig. 24) the grain of bird's-eye maple panels set off within four-square, lightly molded frames, is complemented by inset Japanese hand-painted tiles to emphasize the element of individual craftsmanship that ran contrary to the

Fig. 24, L

growing mechanization of production. As in all other furniture forms of the late 19th century, beds were also made of maple in imitation of bamboo (Fig. 25). It was about the same time that brass bedsteads were widely advertised as highly practical equipment for the home (Fig. 26).

Fig. 25, MMA

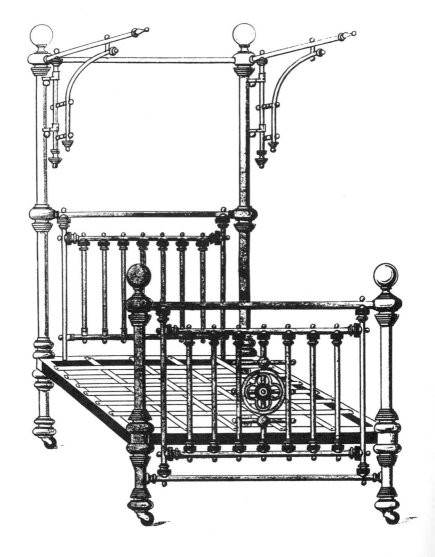

Fig. 26, MMA

XIII

Clocks

If any 17th-century American clocks have survived, the fact has been kept a very dark secret. None have been recorded. However, there were colonial clockmakers during those years and examples of their workmanship conceivably may yet be discovered. It seems likely, on the other hand, that most of the earliest timepieces used in American homes were imported from England and Holland, and even those were apparently an uncommon household luxury.

Small brass clocks known as lantern clocks were among such imports. As in the example shown here (Fig. 1), the circular dial is engraved to indicate the hours but not the minutes, and a single hand suffices to tell the time. The piece is surmounted by a domed bell. Such mechanisms were weight driven and were hung on the wall to allow space for the weights to descend. Pendulums were not introduced until the end of the 17th century, at which time some early models were converted to accommodate the new device, as in the clock illustrated. Examples with such short pendulums are known as "wag on the wall" clocks.

Also among the earlier imports were town clocks brought from overseas and installed in public buildings to be consulted by all the townspeople. One was operating in Boston by 1657. About 1726 a public wall clock was made by two parishioners for the Old North Church in that city, where it is still in use (Fig. 2).

As longer pendulums became customary, tall cases were devised to house and protect the works. (The term "grandfather clock," used to designate these tall case pieces, was derived from a popular song of the 1880s.) Clocks thereupon became the joint product of a cabinetmaker and a clockmaker. Generally speaking, the design of the case followed the furniture styles of the day.

Typical of the earliest tall clocks known to have been made in the colonies, an example with works by John Wood, Sr., of Philadelphia, has a flat top and a rectangular brass dial with applied cast ornaments in the corners (Fig. 3). Two hands tell the minutes as well as the hours, and as an additional refinement, a second, smaller dial reveals the day of the month. Four slender colonettes enframe the glazed hood, which has side windows through which the works may be observed. The piece was probably made about 1730. At approximately the same time, William Claggett of Newport supplied the works for a generally similar timepiece (Fig. 4). One significant difference in design is the superstructure of the hood with its two flanking ball finials, a promise of greater elaboration soon to follow.

The developing nature of that elaboration is apparent in a

Fig. 1, MMA

Fig. 2, ONC

Fig. 3, BG

Fig. 4, BMFA

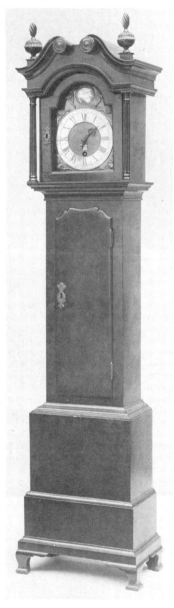

Fig. 6, IS

Fig. 5, MMA

miniature tall case clock with works by Thomas Claggett, son of William (Fig. 5). Here the hood rises in a scroll pediment with the urn finials and twisting flames characteristic of Newport craftsmanship of the middle years of the 18th century. The dial is arched, as would remain customary in years to come. Such smaller versions of tall case clocks are often called grandmother clocks. They stand about five feet tall, whereas the tall ones are often well over seven feet.

The dial of a case clock made by Samuel Bagnall of Boston about the middle of the 18th century shows in detail the arrangement of hour, minute, and second hands typical of the period. In an opening between the hands the day of the month is indicated. Cast ornaments fill the spandrels of the dial and surround the maker's name plate in the arch surmounting the dial proper (Fig. 6).

In the decade preceding the Revolutionary War, the eminent colonial scientist David Rittenhouse supplied the mechanism that was housed in a clock case designed and carved in the finest Philadelphia Chippendale manner (Fig. 7). The silvered brass dial is inscribed by Edward Duffield, friend of Benjamin Franklin. The arch of the dial displays a painted representation of the phases of the moon. Cast rococo ornaments fill the four spandrels of the dial. This is one of the most elaborate of all colonial tall case clocks. It stands in sharp contrast to a very simple, earlier example, also with works by Rittenhouse, made of tulipwood painted to simulate walnut (Fig. 8). The plain round brass dial has no ornament and the construction has neither a shaped pediment nor feet.

Some clocks continued to dispense with cases altogether; the works were merely hung high enough on the wall for the exposed pendulum and weights to clear any obstacle beneath (Fig. 9). Thomas Jefferson hung a clock high in the entrance hall of Monticello, whose works only were enclosed in an architectural hood; it was run by weights made of Revolutionary War cannon balls that were hung down opposite walls of the hall marking the days of the week as they slowly descended (Fig. 10). The walls were not high enough to accommodate the indications for Friday afternoons and Saturdays, so holes were cut through the floor for the weights to pass through and out of sight at the week's end.

Fig. 7, HFdP   Fig. 8, HFdP

During the several decades that followed the Revolutionary War, there was no substantial change in the design of tall clock cases. Probably the most obvious new development was the frequent substitution of painted sheet iron dials (Fig. 11), often imported from England, for the brass dials of earlier years—although these also continued to be used. For the rest, ornament was flat and restrained, largely in the form of inlaid detail. Regional variations in case designs persisted. An example of what is called the "Roxbury" type, made around 1800 by the well-known Massachusetts craftsman Simon Willard, characteristically has a painted dial, fluted corner columns on the waist, bracket feet, an arched head ornamented with scroll work, and vase-shaped brass finials (Fig. 12).

A variation of the basic design is shown in a clock made in New Hampshire about 1815 of local birchwood (Fig. 13). Here a flat-top hood is surmounted by a horizontal openwork fret. A dwarf tall case clock (just four feet in height) made of pine is a country version of the high style (Fig. 14). There is no inlay, the

Fig. 9, OS

Fig. 10, TJMF

Fig. 11, IS

Fig. 12, BMFA

Fig. 13, BMFA

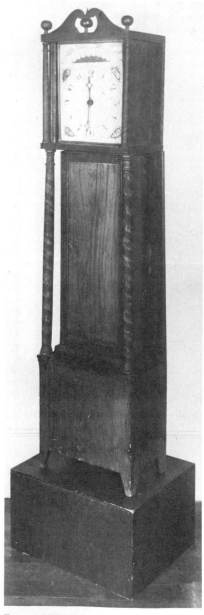

Fig. 14, NYSHA   Fig. 15, HFM

pediment and finials are rudimentary in form; the simple columns are free standing, the dial is painted on the back of a glass panel, leaving the hands exposed; and the works are made of wood. Another dwarf tall case clock—it is only three feet tall—was made about 1800 by Benjamin Seth Youngs of Watervliet, New York (Fig. 15). The Shakers had a community at Watervliet and the very simple pine case of this clock and its undecorated dial reflect the unpretentious, straightforward craftsmanship characteristic of all Shaker-made products.

By the 1830s grandfather and grandmother clocks were passing out of fashion. Smaller, and when possible, less expensive timepieces were in increasing demand.

Spring-driven clocks designed to stand on brackets or tables were occasionally made in America in the late colonial period and, somewhat more commonly, in the years following the Revolution. Figure 16 represents an example encased in walnut veneer and fitted with a handle at the top and mounted on small feet, apparently made in New York about 1775. Another example

Fig. 16, HFM

Fig. 17, HFdP

Fig. 18, BMFA   Fig. 19, BMFA

standing on a bracket made to accommodate it was also made in
New York in the closing years of the 18th century (Fig. 17). Both
clocks are similar in style to those made in England and imported
to America.

It was in these same years that American clockmaking took a
new and vital turn with the development of small and relatively
inexpensive timepieces of a distinctively native character, clocks
that also avoided the problems of spring-motivated movements.
An early example representing this trend is the Massachusetts wall
clock made around 1780–90 by Simon Willard to simulate a small
clock standing on a matching bracket (Fig. 18). Actually, the case
consists of a box on a box, the upper one housing the mechanism
and the lower one accommodating the weights and the swinging
pendulum (Fig. 19). What is known as the Massachusetts shelf
clock, another small model, remained popular from just before
and through several decades after the Revolution. It was made in a
variety of designs over the years. An early example, made about

Fig. 20, BG   Fig. 21, OS

1790 with works by David Wood of Newburyport, Massachusetts,
is illustrated in Figure 20. The box-on-box arrangement reduced
to very simple terms is shown in an example made in New Hampshire about 1790 (Fig. 21). A balloon-shaped opening in the pine
case reveals a round brass dial with a cutout to show the revolving
hours, and, on the lower exposure, the name of the maker, Levi
Hutchins. In later years, with changing styles in the decorative
arts, clocks of this general type took on a more elaborate appearance. In an example made about 1820 by Aaron Willard, the
painted decoration of the glass panels follows the height of fashion
of the Empire period (Fig. 22), as do the brass feet in the form of
lions' paws (Fig. 23).

In the early years of the 19th century Willard also supplied
gallery clocks for several churches and other public buildings in
Boston and its neighborhood. They usually took the form of the
example illustrated (Fig. 24), which measures slightly more than
three-and-a-half feet in height. About this time, also, consign-

Fig. 22, BMFA

Fig. 23, BMFA

Fig. 24, BMFA

Fig. 25, MMA

ments of gilt-bronze shelf or mantel clocks with the free-standing figure of George Washington and otherwise adorned with patriotic motifs relating to his fame were imported from France (Fig. 25). The figure was modeled on a portrait of Washington by John Trumbull.

In 1802 Simon Willard invented his "Improved Patent Time piece," as he called it—the eight-day banjo clock that won immediate success and that was quickly copied by other makers, despite his patent. With its gilt case, painted glass panels and delicate hands—and above all, its precise workmanship and fine proportions—its popularity was well deserved. The glass panels of such clocks were often elaborately and colorfully painted. On its lower panel, an example made about 1810–25 by one of Willard's apprentices depicts a view of Boston Common (Fig. 26). The gilt bracket with applied pendant balls was a frequent embellishment. In a slightly later variation of the banjo, the center section of the case takes the shape of a lyre (Fig. 27), a motif widely used in

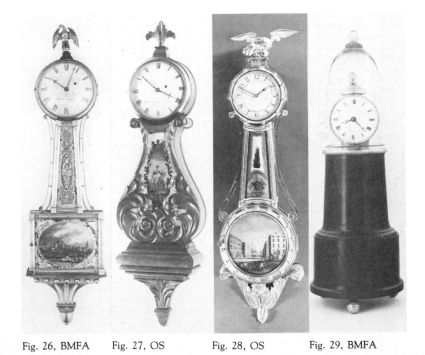

Fig. 26, BMFA   Fig. 27, OS   Fig. 28, OS   Fig. 29, BMFA

furniture of the classical revival period. Lyre clocks were made, chiefly by Massachusetts craftsmen, with varying ornamental detail, from about 1820 until about the middle of the century.

Another, more elaborate, variant of the banjo style was the girandole clock developed by Lemuel Curtis of Concord, Massachusetts and Burlington, Vermont, about 1815 and so called because its convex circular bottom section resembled the girandole looking glasses of the empire period (Fig. 28). These convex surfaces are customarily handsomely painted with city views, landscape scenes, mythological subjects, and the like. Such clocks are widely considered the most beautiful examples of American clockmaking—and they have often been copied, with and without intention to deceive.

In 1822 Willard also patented his lighthouse clock (Fig. 29)—the "Eddystone Lighthouse Alarm Time piece," named after the famous structure built upon the Eddystone Rocks, near Plymouth, England. Although when it appeared the model was not as popular as his banjo clock, it is still admired and collected. The glass dome

Fig. 30, HFM

Fig. 31, HFM

of such timepieces is removable for the weekly winding, the "alarm set" is at the center of the case, and the silvered alarm bell is suspended above. Almost no two of the surviving examples are exactly alike in detail.

As already observed in the introduction to this book, the Yankee invention early in the 19th century of producing clock works with machine-made, interchangeable parts in an assembly line factory revolutionized the industry. At the same time veneer and mortising mills and circular saws reduced the cost of the cases far below former levels. One report from Hartford, Connecticut, in 1841 boasted that by then five hundred thousand inexpensive clocks were being manufactured yearly in that state alone.

The first pillar-and-scroll clocks that were early examples of such enterprise were turned out by Eli Terry about 1816 and were produced by him and many others until about 1840. Although there were variations in the design, typically the case of this form of clock stands on slender feet, with flanking pillars and a broken-arch or double-scroll pediment; the glass panels are frequently painted with landscape scenes (Fig. 30).

As the mid-century approached, a wide variety of clock cases were designed to house mass-produced works. Coiled springs priced at seventy-five cents or less were now being manufactured in New England. Among the new forms that no longer needed to accommodate weight-driven works was the acorn clock (Fig. 31), a type made in the 1840s by Jonathan Clark Brown in Bristol, Connecticut. The painted lower panels of these sinuously shaped models frequently represented landscapes of primitive charm.

More traditional designs took on characteristics of the new and changing styles in decoration. By the 1830s shelf clocks in the pillar-and-scroll manner were losing their earlier lightness in favor of bolder details in the Empire style. Pillars, or columns, became stouter and scrolls flatter and less delicately arched. As in the case of other furniture forms of the period, stencilled designs were used to suggest remotely the applied gilded metal decorations used on fine French Empire furniture (Fig. 32). Alternatively, these elements were heavily carved in patterns characteristic of the period (Fig. 33). Another type of clock case that could be very loosely said to be in the Empire style, the looking-glass, or mirror, clock was made principally in New Hampshire in the 1820s. In one

Fig. 32, OS

Fig. 33, NGA

Fig. 34, HFM

Fig. 35, WRHS

Fig. 36, OS

Fig. 38, HFM

Fig. 37

Fig. 39, HFM

Fig. 40, HFM

representative example of about 1830 the rectangular frame is constructed of half-round columns turned in a single pattern of gilded rings alternating with slightly bulbous elements (Fig. 34). The upper section within the frame displays a clock face; the lower section consists of a looking glass. A lyre-shaped wall clock made about 1845 shows the Empire style in its last phase (Fig. 35). Here the design is reduced to a sawed profile that is both simply executed and attractive.

Around this time—the 1840s—the so-called steeple clock won wide popularity (Fig. 36). Obviously designed in the spirit of the Gothic-revival style of the time, these very successful shelf clocks were produced in many variations, but always with primary emphasis on the "steeple." Many of them survive today.

From the forties until the end of the century, many varieties of clocks were designed and developed. One exceedingly popular type, the "O-G," or ogee, clock is so called because of the double curve of its broad, simply molded frame, a contour known as an ogee or ogival design (Fig. 37). Ogee clocks were made in all sizes and with various kinds of works, usually with painted glass panels in the lower section, throughout most of the rest of the century. A representative example (Fig. 38) dates from about 1850.

Every passing style and fashion during the second half of the 19th century added to the proliferation of different types of clocks. Many of them were now made by large manufacturing concerns, and they all reflected the eclectic tastes of the time. About 1855 the American Clock Co. of New York produced a cast-iron model with Gothic crockets and cusped arches topping an arrangement of classical figures, urns and columns, and a romantic landscape (Fig. 39). Also in the 1850s, other firms were manufacturing cases of papier-mâché with mother-of-pearl inlay and painted decoration—decoration that can be best and most simply described as Victorian (Fig. 40).

The increase in railroad travel called for precise station clocks, such as the tall-case example made about 1860 shown in Figure 41. In its style, the carved walnut case is related to other furniture forms of the Renaissance-revival period. (As an adjunct to these, painted signs indicating departures of trains were posted at prominent spots in the station [Fig. 42].)

There was apparently no limit to the range of prices and styles.

Fig. 41, WRHS

Fig. 42, S

Fig. 43, HFM

Fig. 44, HM

By the 1860s mass-produced one-day brass clocks were being made at a cost of less than fifty cents each. Others were custom-made at considerable expense. Machine-made cases in modified versions of the Renaissance-revival and other current styles were turned out in great quantities and in many variant forms, one of which is illustrated in Figure 43. Some were candidly made for use in the kitchen. Demonstrations of jig-sawing at the Philadelphia Centennial encouraged even amateurs to fashion their own clock cases (Fig. 44)—and almost everything else. Other novelties of the 1860s and 1870s included cases made of cast iron in the form of curious human and animal figures whose eyes would mechanically blink with the passage of the seconds (Fig. 45), reminiscent of the automata of the late Middle Ages and the Renaissance.

Hardly less remarkable were the very fashionable timepieces turned out by the more important jewelers in major cities, who employed clockmakers to complement their especially designed

Fig. 45, WRHS   Fig. 46, L

cases. An example in marble and bronze, resembling a fanciful miniature cathedral, was made by the Philadelphia firm of Baily Banks and Biddle as the center piece of a mantel garniture (Fig. 46). Even more fanciful is a case in an imagined Oriental style made for the New York home of John D. Rockefeller, Sr. (Fig. 47). In the 1880s Tiffany and Company produced an extraordinary clock in the Near Eastern style that is probably the last word in eclecticism (Fig. 48). The case is topped by a brass dome ornamented with stars and crescents, following Turkish, Persian and Indian models, the dials show the year, month, period of the

Fig. 47, MCNY   Fig. 48, MMA

zodiac, phases of the moon and sun, date, and day of the week, as well as the hour, minute, and second. A pendulum containing mercury suspended on a brass rod regulates the movement, regardless of fluctuations of temperature or barometric pressure.

About that same time, a customer with less extravagant notions could have bought an inexpensive alarm clock in the most modern style from Sears, Roebuck for next to nothing (Fig. 49). At the World's Columbian Exposition in Chicago, 1892–93, "Columbus wall clocks" reminiscent of the lantern clocks of earlier centuries were offered for sale as souvenirs (Fig. 50). They were made in Ohio and bore a crude medallion portrait of Christopher Columbus and the date 1492.

Those who promoted the Mission style made tall clocks in which the elaborate cases of earlier years were reduced to an almost skeletal simplicity of plain, square-sectioned upright members (Fig. 51).

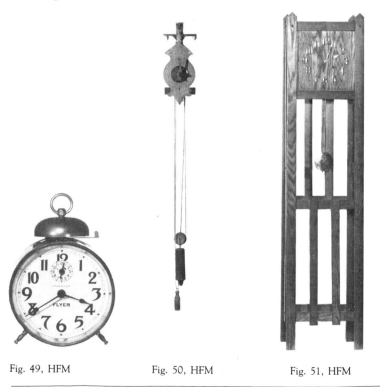

Fig. 49, HFM   Fig. 50, HFM   Fig. 51, HFM

XIV

Looking Glasses

T he earliest looking glasses that have survived from colonial America date from the William and Mary period. In all probability most of them were imported from England. A typical example is of rectangular shape, relatively small and with a convex molded frame of walnut veneer (Fig. 1). Occasionally the frame was topped by an intricately pierced ("seaweed") cresting (Fig. 2) that recalls the crests of the tall-back chairs of the period (Fig. 3).

Fig. 1, WA

Fig. 2, MMA

Fig. 3

Fig. 4, IS   Fig. 5, HFM   Fig. 6, HFdP

Fig. 7, HFdP

Fig. 8, HFM

Fig. 9, MMA

Those early styles were faintly echoed much later in the 18th century when what are known as courting mirrors were introduced, probably as imports from northern Europe. A frame with a similar bold molding and with an angular crest has an inner lining of crudely painted glass insets that encloses the reflecting glass (Fig. 4). These relatively small forms were originally fitted into a shallow box with a sliding cover.

In the Queen Anne period that followed, taller glasses were often used. Sheets of glass were then made from blown cylinders that were split and flattened while the glass was still hot enough from its firing to be thus manipulated. The process necessarily limited their size, hence the piecing together of two (and sometimes three) sections, as in the example illustrated (Fig. 5) from the second quarter of the century. The top section was frequently engraved in an ornamental pattern, and a carved and gilded shell ornamented the cresting.

In this period the outlines of looking glasses assumed more

Fig. 10, HFdP

Fig. 11, MMA

decorative shapes, with scrolled elements at top and bottom, that gave the form new importance as a household accessory (Fig. 6). To increase their usefulness, looking glasses frequently were fitted with brass sconces, or candle holders, attached to the bottom scrolls, as these appear on a long horizontal example made about 1720–30—a "chimney looking glass," intended for a place above the mantel of a fireplace (Fig. 7). In this case the reflecting glass is composed of three sections surrounded by a carved and gilded molding, an increasingly common embellishment. It was during the Queen Anne period that the dressing glass, or toilet mirror—a small looking glass supported by uprights and mounted on a miniature stand with drawers (Fig. 8)—was introduced to colonial America. Judging from the very few known examples dating from pre-Revolutionary times, the form was rarely produced during those years, although it became relatively popular in postwar decades.

As the 18th century advanced toward the Chippendale period,

Fig. 12, PMA   Fig. 13, BMFA

looking glasses, like case pieces, frequently exhibited an architectural character (Fig. 9), with moldings and scrolls duplicating those of doors, windows, and cornices of the rooms in which they were hung. And like those other types of furniture—secretaries, highboys, and clocks—as the height of rooms increased, looking glasses could take taller shapes.

The scrolled outline of the Queen Anne style continued into the Chippendale period with somewhat more ornate gilded carving reflecting the influence of the rococo (Fig. 10). A variety of glasses dating from the decades immediately before and after the Revolution display that influence in more emphatic ways. The frame of one example, made in Philadelphia around 1765 and typical of the most developed stage of rococo ornament, is composed almost entirely of carved and gilded C scrolls and other characteristic curved and floral motifs enclosing small panels of glass surrounding the main glass (Fig. 11). Plates in the pattern books of Chippendale and other contemporary English designers provided ready models for the guidance of American craftsmen. Sometimes these published designs were followed almost literally,

Fig. 14, HFdP

as in the example just cited; at other times they were worked into simplified adaptations by provincial craftsmen, as in the case of the glass illustrated in Figure 12. The ingeniously designed cresting of the frame of this example, with two reversed hearts and a stylized tulip, is a translation of Chippendale formulas into the Pennsylvania-German dialect. (The swirling swastika on the apron originated in the ancient world as a symbol for the sun.)

With the introduction of classical revival styles late in the 18th century, looking glasses assumed lighter and more delicate forms. The production of the carved and gilded frames typical of the Federal period called for specialized skills in the use of composition and wired ornament and gold leaf—and it was costly work. It is by no means always possible to determine whether such glasses were actually made in this country or imported from England. In either case the designs were similar. The example shown here (Fig. 13), produced in New England, closely resembles the designs published by Hepplewhite in his *Guide*. The ornamental scrolls with leaf and flower motifs are made of wire covered with "French putty," or gesso, that, like the frame itself, is carved and gilded.

A large gilded overmantel looking glass in the Sheraton style— it measures more than six feet across—was made in Albany or New York City about 1805 (Fig. 14). The fringe of small balls and the slender colonettes are typical elements of early 19th century frames. They very frequently appear on what are called tabernacle mirrors, a Sheraton-style form that retained its popularity through the second decade of the century. Above the reflecting glass of such pieces a wood or glass panel with painted or relief decoration often represents a patriotic theme (Fig. 15). In a fairly large number of examples the basic Chippendale form was carried over into the classical revival period, but with a refinement of details that characterizes the changing fashion. The scrolled pediment of a looking glass in the Hepplewhite style, for instance, takes a more delicate shape than its Chippendale forerunners (Fig. 16). Its gilt vase with graceful branching tendrils and its discreet inlay also reflect the new spirit in design.

For the last fifty years or so, looking glasses with frames of marble mosaic veneer have been generally termed Bilbao mirrors (Fig. 17). It is presumed they were imported into this country around the turn of the 18th century, possibly brought here by

Fig. 15, MMA

Fig. 16, HFM

Fig. 17, MMA

Fig. 18, HFM

Fig. 19, CW

Fig. 20, BMFA

Fig. 21, MMA

American merchant ships that used the Spanish town of Bilbao as a port of call and where such mirrors could be bought.

In his *Dictionary* of 1803, Sheraton observed that mirrors with convex glasses in circular gilt frames had become "universally fashionable." The fashion quickly spread to the newly formed United States. Like the convex reflectors today used as aids to security in stores, lobbies, and elevators, these glasses brought a view of almost an entire room into a small focus. Often called girandoles (a word which originally meant a branched candlestick), these forms, as in the example illustrated (Fig. 18), customarily have scrolled candle branches, concave frames lined with gilt balls, and decorations of carved foliage. The carved eagle that so frequently perches on a pedestal surmounting such a piece represents a decorative device that has been popular for centuries and has no necessary reference to any American bird, bald eagle, or otherwise.

It was during the years of the early Republic that the dressing glass enjoyed its greatest vogue. These small pieces with small adjustable glasses suspended between vertical supports, with or without drawers, were later replaced by similar swiveling glasses that were an integral part of a bureau (see Chapter VI). Figure 19 represents the most typical form of dressing glass made in America during the Federal period. A most elegant example made in Salem about 1790–1800 has an elliptical base with drawers, the whole case composed of alternating bands of mahogany and satinwood and the frame supporting the glass of carved and gilded mahogany (Fig. 20). A Chinese version made from the same period, made of black and gold lacquer, for the export trade to the Western world, follows the occidental style in its own exotic fashion (Fig. 21).

Small portable mirrors with round frames and turned or shaped handles (Fig. 22) apparently were commonly to be seen on early 19th century dressing tables.

Fig. 22, HFdP

Taller, free-standing looking glasses, sometimes known as "swingers" but more commonly termed cheval glasses, were also made for providing a more complete view of a person. An example dating from the early years of the 19th century (Fig. 23) corresponds to what Sheraton described as "a kind of tall dressing-glass" which "may when hung by two centre screws, be turned back or forward to suit the person who dresses at them."

As in the case of many other kinds of furnishings, the increased use of cast iron encouraged novel designs in looking glasses. In a popular model of the 1850s two flounced and hooped ladies perched on willow tree branches hold an oval glass in an ornate frame topped by a pair of gamboling cherubs swinging a wreath.

Fig. 23, HFdP   Fig. 24, SHR

An obelisk rising from the base is flanked by such symbols as an American flag, a sheath of arrows, and an olive branch (Fig. 24). The same type of mirror was made at many foundries in the 1850s when P. T. Barnum was selling the Swedish Nightingale to the American public and they are consequently called "Jenny Lind" mirrors. Figure 25 represents another cast-iron form produced at about the same time, also by several different manufacturers. The resemblance of the cast ornament to furniture carvings of the

Fig. 25, SHR   Fig. 26, SHR

rococo-revival period is obvious, as it is in the cast-iron umbrella, hat, and coat rack with mirror from about the same time (Fig. 26).

An elegant counterpart of this manner of decoration is illustrated in a gilt pier glass (Fig. 27) made in 1853 as part of a parlor suite of furnishings for a new home in Massachusetts. Here the rococo-style leafy scrolls are delicately fashioned and combined with a spiral twist molding often used in the period. A complete change in fashion is shown in a huge hanging glass (it is more than seven feet tall) made at New York in 1876 (Fig. 28). It represents a revived Jacobean pattern, a giant version of the small octagonal looking glasses made in England during the 1600s. The beveled framework is ornamented with intricate inlays, as recommended by Eastlake in cases "where an effect of greater richness is aimed at."

Fig. 27, MMA   Fig. 28, PMA

For more intimate reflections gentlemen of the 1880s could resort to face-high adjustable mirrors mounted on tall shaving stands (Fig. 29). About this time, as a further convenience, they could use the newly devised safety razor ("No practice required. Impossible to cut the face.").

Fig. 29, HFM

XV

Candlestands & Firescreens

The first truly adequate lighting device was invented in 1783 by the Swiss Aimé Argand, a lamp that was the parent form of the subsequent improved oil lamps. Throughout all earlier history, and in many areas for years still to come, for light at night man had to depend on such weak sources of illumination as primitive oil lamps, flammable rushes, candles, or the flickering flames of a fire in the hearth.

Devices for holding or supporting candles and candlesticks were among the indispensable furnishings of colonial homes. One such, actually a primitive form of rush holder, is nothing more than a wrought-iron clamp fixed in a simple but solid cone of wood, dating from the late 17th century (Fig. 1). An ingenious adjustable candlestand, also mounted on a crude wooden block, has a ratchet by means of which the candle may be raised or lowered (Fig. 2). Still another example has a threaded shaft for adjusting to the required height both an arm supporting two candles and a circular tray beneath (Fig. 3).

Throughout the 18th century, local woodworkers turned out a wide variety of stands, usually of pine and maple, to hold separate candlesticks made of pewter, brass, silver, or whatever (Figs. 4, 5, 6). The character of the turnings of the upright support is the major element that determines their interest. One early example of especial note in this regard stands on trestle feet with a well-turned vase-shaped stretcher connecting the equally well-turned legs (Fig. 7). Obviously it was fashioned to accommodate a number of sticks which could be drawn from for placement wherever else they might be needed.

Meanwhile, urban craftsmen were producing more sophisticated stands in the Queen Anne and Chippendale styles,

Fig. 1, MMA   Fig. 2, HFdP

fashioned of walnut or mahogany. One such is distinguishable from a fashionable tripod tea table of the time—about the middle of the 18th century—only by the small size of its dish top; it is just twenty inches in diameter (Fig. 8). With its so-called bird-cage arrangement, the top could be turned and tilted. Made about the same time, another candlestand also provides a wooden screen as a guard from the competing glare and the direct heat of the fire (Fig.

Fig. 3, WA

Fig. 4, MMA   Fig. 5, WA   Fig. 6, AIC

Fig. 7, WA

Fig. 8, HFM   Fig. 9, HFdP

9). One contemporary record referred to what was probably a similar piece as a "Screen Candlestick."

An unusual, tall, and elegantly designed and carved tripod candlestand, made about 1778, has the elongated ball-and-claw feet characteristic of Massachusetts craftsmanship of the Chippendale period (Fig. 10). The shaft is in the form of a fluted Corinthian column.

Fire screens were made separately. The mahogany standard and legs of one example are turned and curved in the manner of Newport craftsmanship in the Chippendale period; its adjustable screen is covered by an embroidered panel, a not uncommon practice of the time—and of years later (Fig. 11). Another pole screen, as such forms are and were sometimes termed, dating from the middle years of the 18th century, has a solid wooden panel that may be raised or lowered at need (Fig. 12).

The popularity of these types of furniture lasted as long as people depended upon open fires and candlelight for their comforts and conveniences. As Sheraton observed in his *Drawing Book* (1793), a lady needed some such convenience that she "may both receive the benefit of the fire, and have her face screened from its scorching heat." The varieties shown in both his and Hepplewhite's books are suggested by a few representative examples shown here. That shown in Figure 13, made around the turn of the century, has a drop-leaf tray which when raised supported a candle. The tripod

Fig. 10, HFdP   Fig. 11, MMA

cabriole base recalls the designs of Chippendale, although the legs are more delicately contoured than they would have been earlier. Such delicacy is even more pronounced in one of a pair of Sheraton-style pole screens, made about 1800–10, with a dainty floral print framed in its relatively small panel (Fig. 14).

Two candlestands from the Federal period, one with a fixed top (Fig. 15), and the other with a larger, tilting top (Fig. 16), reflect the refinement of design, carving, and inlay typical of the best of

Fig. 12, BMFA   Fig. 13, BMFA

New England workmanship of the early 19th century. In both cases the apparent simplicity of the forms clearly expresses the classical spirit as it was interpreted in this country.

Sheraton's published designs provided models for the fireside desk shown in Figure 17, probably made in New York in the late 18th century. The hinged door of this shallow piece drops down to provide a writing surface, while the solid back serves as protection from the fire's glare.

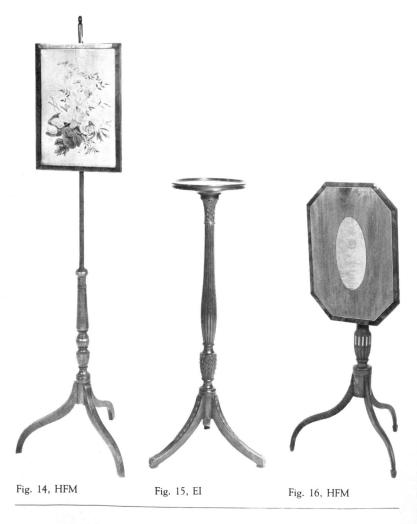

Fig. 14, HFM   Fig. 15, EI   Fig. 16, HFM

With the introduction of various other types of lighting devices, the use of candles gradually diminished except as a pleasant accent when bright lighting was not required.

The panel of a fashionable firescreen of the 1880s is covered by needlework depicting a sentimental subject typical of late Victorian taste. The walnut frame is ornamented by incised gilded designs and shallow carving of the sort widely employed on other furniture forms of the period (Fig. 18).

Fig. 17, SHR   Fig. 18, NM

Glossary

Apron	The horizontal wooden strip directly beneath the frames of a chair seat, a table top, a looking glass, or the body of a case piece, frequently carved, pieced, or otherwise decoratively treated; also called a skirt or skirting
Baluster	An upright support of a rail, usually turned in the shape of a slender vase
Block front	The front of a case piece in which a receding center section is flanked by two blocklike projecting sections
Bonnet top	A broken-scroll pediment forming a continuous hood from front to back of a tall case piece of furniture
Boss	An applied convex ornament oval or circular in outline and often colored in contrast to the background of a chest or cupboard
Brad molding	A molding of conjoined semispherical elements suggesting a string of beads
Breakfront	A secretary or bookcase with a protruding central section
Cabriole	A type of furniture leg curved outward at the knee and inward below and terminating in a shaped foot
Case furniture	Any piece of furniture of box- or caselike character, such as a chest of drawers, secretary, bookcase, or whatever
Cornice	The uppermost, projecting molding at the top of a large case piece, a window, or a wall

Crest rail	The top rail of a crest, sofa or other form of seating furniture
Dished top	The top of a table with raised edges resembling the rim or lip of a dish
Dowel	A wooden peg or pin, usually rounded, inserted into holes in two adjoining pieces of wood to fasten them together and align them
Fretwork	A decorative design resembling a lattice, either freestanding, applied, or cut in low relief
Gallery	A small balustrade or strip of open fretwork forming a railing that edges the top of a piece of furniture
Jewelwork	Ornamental carving resembling cut gems
Matting	A coarsely tooled surface resembling a rough fabric, often used as a background to set off a more highly finished ornament
Mortise and Tenon	The method of joining two pieces of wood by inserting an extension of one piece (tenon) into a socket (mortise) of the other, and usually further securing by a hardwood pin or dowel piercing both pieces
Ormolu	More or less ornate gilded brass or bronze mounts applied to furniture; most commonly associated with French furniture and its derivations
Pediment	An arched or triangular section surmounting the entablature of an architectural or furniture form in the classical manner
Rail	The horizontal member of a chair seat supported by the legs
Reeding	A decorative motif of slender semicircular elements carved in relief and resembling straight, grouped reeds
Skirt	See apron

Spandrel	The triangular space enclosed by the curve of an arch and the rectangular framework surrounding it
Spindle	A slender, turned upright used primarily as a support of a chair back
Splat	The flat, central, upright elements of a chair back, either solid or pieced
Stile	The upright side supports of a chair back
Strapwork	A design consisting of flat interlaced bands applied to or carved on the surface of a piece of furniture
Stretcher	The horizontal support joining and bracing the legs of a table, chair, or other furniture form
Tambour	A flexible sliding door made of thin strips of wood glued to a canvas backing
Trestle table	A table with a framework of horizontal crosspieces joined by vertical supports
Turning	A process in which pieces of wood are symmetrically shaped or cut while turning on a lathe, as used for making legs, spindles, stretchers, and so forth

Bibliography

Andrews, Edward D., and Faith, *Shaker Furniture*. New Haven, 1950.

Bishop, Robert, *The American Chair*. New York, 1972.

Bjerhoe, Ethel Hall, *The Cabinetmakers of America*. Garden City, N.Y., 1957.

Bridenbaugh, Carl, *The Colonial Craftsman*. New York, 1950.

Burton, E. Milby, *Charleston Furniture, 1700–1825*. Charleston, 1955.

Butler, Joseph T., *American Antiques, 1800–1900*. New York, 1965.

Butler, Joseph T., *American Furniture*. London, 1973.

Carpenter, Ralph E., Jr., *The Arts and Crafts of Newport, Rhode Island, 1640–1820*. Preservation Society of Newport County, 1954.

Comstock, Helen, *American Furniture*. New York, 1962.

Comstock, Helen, *The Looking Glass in America, 1700–1825*. New York, 1968.

Davidson, Marshall B., *Colonial Antiques*. New York, 1967.

Davidson, Marshall B., *American Antiques from the Revolution to the Civil War*. New York, 1968.

Davidson, Marshall B., *Antiques from the Civil War to World War I*. New York, 1969.

Distin, William H., and Bishop, Robert, *The American Clock*. New York, 1976.

Downs, Joseph, *American Furniture, Queen Anne and Chippendale Periods*. New York, 1952.

Dreppard, Carl W., *The Primer of American Antiques*. New York, 1944.

Dreppard, Carl W., *Dictionary of Antiques*. New York, 1953.

Durant, Mary, *American Heritage Guide to Antiques*. New York, 1970.

Fales, Dean A., Jr., *American Painted Furniture, 1660–1880*. New York, 1972.

Hornor, William M., Jr., *Blue Book, Philadelphia Furniture*.

Metropolitan Museum of Art, *19th Century America—Furniture and Decorative Arts*. New York, 1970.

Montgomery, Charles, *American Furniture: The Federal Period*. New York, 1966.

Nutting, Wallace, *Furniture Treasury*. New York, 1948.

Otto, Celia Jackson, *American Furniture of the Nineteenth Century*. New York, 1965.

Ormsbee, Thomas H., *Field Guide to American Victorian Furniture*. New York, 1952.

Randall, Richard H., Jr., *American Furniture in the Museum of Fine Arts, Boston*. Boston, 1965.

Winchester, Alice, *How to Know American Antiques*. New York, 1951.

Index

Photo Credits

AAAM—Anglo-American Art Museum: Chests of Drawers, Fig. 19

ACCNY—Art Commission, City of New York: Desks, Fig. 32

AIC—Art Institute of Chicago: Historical Introduction, Fig. 15; Chairs, Fig. 55; Chests & Boxes, Fig. 35; Cupboards, Fig. 6; Candlestands, Fig. 6

AIHA—Albany Institute of History and Art: Chairs, Fig. 34; Tables, Figs. 9, 20; Beds, Fig. 17

BC—Bowdoin College Museum of Art: Historical Introduction, Fig. 1

BG—Benjamin Ginsburg: Chairs, Figs. 44, 73; Highboys & Lowboys, Fig. 14; Tables, Fig. 3; Dining Furniture, Fig. 9; Beds, Fig. 16; Clocks, Figs. 3, 20

BM—Brooklyn Museum: Chairs, Figs. 20, 101, 108; Cupboards, Figs. 22, 28; Desks, Fig. 48; Tables, Fig. 26; Beds, Fig. 19

BMA—Baltimore Museum of Art: Tables, Fig. 42

BMFA—Museum of Fine Arts, Boston: Historical Introduction, Figs. 12, 23, 32, 37; Chairs, Figs. 1, 56; Chests & Boxes, Figs. 1, 3, 5, 12, 15, 33; Highboys & Lowboys, Figs. 6, 9; Chests of Drawers, Figs. 1, 4, 7, 8, 9, 10, 12, 16, 17, 18; Dressers & Bureaus, Figs. 1, 2; Cupboards, Figs. 1, 2, 3; Desks, Figs. 8, 14, 19, 20, 21, 26, 29; Tables, Figs. 17, 27, 29, 30, 33; Dining Furniture, Figs. 5, 7, 10, 11, 15; Clocks, Figs. 4, 12, 13, 18, 19, 22, 23, 24, 26, 29; Looking Glasses, Figs. 13, 20; Candlestands, Figs. 12, 13

CHS—Connecticut Historical Society: Chairs, Figs. 8, 47

CU—Cooper Union: Chairs, Fig. 77

CW—Colonial Williamsburg: Desks, Fig. 5; Dining Furniture, Fig 12; Beds, Figs. 3, 4; Looking Glasses, Fig. 19

EI—Essex Institute, Salem, MA: Candlestands, Fig. 15

FAMS—Fine Arts Museum of the South: Dining Furniture, Fig. 17

GRPM—Grand Rapids Public Museum: Historical Introduction, Fig. 51; Desks, Figs. 46, 47; Tables, Fig. 47

HCHS—Harris County Heritage Society: Dressers & Bureaus, Fig. 7

HD—Historic Deerfield, Inc.: Chests of Drawers, Fig. 14; Desks, Fig. 17

MESDA—Museum of Early Southern Decorative Arts, Winston-Salem, N.C.: Chests of Drawers, Fig. 15

MHS—Missouri Historical Society: Chairs, Fig. 16; Cupboards, Fig. 12

MMA—Metropolitan Museum of Art: Historical Introduction, Figs. 8, 19, 20, 31, 33, 34, 35, 44, 48, 55; Chairs, Figs. 3, 4, 6, 11, 12, 24, 31, 36, 38, 41, 45, 70, 72, 97, 107; Chests & Boxes, Figs. 6, 14, 34; Highboys & Lowboys, Figs. 1, 10, 11, 12, 13; Dressers & Bureaus, Figs. 11, 12; Cupboards, Figs. 4, 5, 16; Desks, Figs. 3, 16; Tables, Figs. 1, 7, 15, 18, 35, 54, 56; Daybeds, Figs. 2, 5, 6, 9, 12; Dining Furniture, Figs. 2, 8, 19; Beds, Figs. 25, 26; Clocks, Figs, 1, 5, 25, 48; Looking Glasses, Figs. 2, 9, 11, 15, 17, 21, 27; Candlestands, Figs. 1, 11

MWPI—Munson-Williams-Proctor Institute: Dressers & Bureaus, Fig. 3; Desks, Figs. 35, 43, 44; Tables, Fig. 44; Dining Furniture, Fig. 4

NGA—National Gallery of Art, Washington, D.C.: Historical Introduction, Fig. 9; Chairs, Figs. 57, 94; Chests & Boxes, Fig. 13; Cupboards, Figs. 11, 20; Desks, Fig. 1; Clocks, Fig. 33

NM—Newark Museum: Historical Introduction, Fig. 36; Dressers & Bureaus, Fig. 8; Desks, Fig. 45; Tables, Figs. 37, 46, 48; Dining Furniture, Fig. 24; Candlestands, Fig. 18

NHHS—New Hampshire Historical Society: Chairs, Figs. 27, 28, 29

N-YHS—New-York Historical Society: Historical Introduction, Figs. 46, 49; Desks, Fig. 15; Tables, Fig. 40

NYPL—New York Public Library: Historical Introduction, Fig. 50; Chairs, Fig. 79; Cupboards, Fig. 27

NYSHA—New York State Historical Assn.: Clocks, Fig. 14

ONC—Old North Church, Boston: Clocks, Fig. 2

OS—Old Sturbridge: Historical Introduction, Fig. 5; Chests & Boxes, Fig. 9; Chest of Drawers, Fig. 3; Cupboards, Fig. 18; Desks, Fig. 40; Clocks, Figs. 9, 21, 27, 28, 32, 36

OSR—Old Salem Restoration, Winston-Salem, N.C.: Chairs, Fig. 35

PC—Private Collection: Chairs, Fig. 76

PHS—Pensacola Historical Society: Desks, Fig. 42

PMA—Philadelphia Museum of Art: Historical Introduction, Figs. 18, 21, 28; Chairs, Figs. 17, 52, 89; Cupboards, Figs. 8, 10, 23; Desks, Fig. 38; Tables, Figs. 23, 24, 25; Daybeds, Fig. 13; Dining Furniture, Fig. 6; Looking Glasses, Figs. 12, 28

PMS—Peabody Museum of Salem: Chairs, Fig. 71

ABOUT THE AUTHOR

MARSHALL B. DAVIDSON has broad and deep experience in the field of American antiques. In 1935 he became Assistant Curator and later Associate Curator of the American Wing of the Metropolitan Museum of Art. In 1947 he became the museum's Editor of Publications. He joined American Heritage Publishing Company in 1961 as Editor of *Horizon* magazine and later was Senior Editor in charge of preparation of books in the fields of art and history.

A prolific writer, Marshall Davidson is the author of *Life in America*, *The American Heritage History of American Antiques*, *The American Heritage History of Notable American Houses*, *The Artist's America*, *The World in 1776*, *A Pictorial History of Architecture in America*, among other books, as well as numerous articles for *Art in America*, *Antiques* magazine, the *New York Times*, *Vogue*, *American Heritage*, *Horizon*, and the publications of the Metropolitan Museum of Art. In 1980 the Metropolitan Museum of Art will publish his complete guide to the collections in the new American Wing of the museum.